Tim Rowland's
Creature Features

Also by Tim

High Peaks Publishing

All Pets are Off: A Collection of Hairy Columns
Petrified Fact: Stories of Bizarre Behavior that Really
Happened, Mostly
Earth to Hagerstown

The History Press

High Peaks: A History of Hiking the Adirondacks from
Noah to Neoprene
Maryland's Appalachian Highlands: Massacres,
Moonshine & Mountaineering

Skyhorse Publishing

Strange and Obscure Stories of the Civil War

Tim Rowland's
Creature Features

Berkeley Springs, West Virginia

Tim Rowland's Creature Features

© 2012 Tim Rowland

Published in the United States of America by
High Peaks Publishing
811 Duckwall Road
Berkeley Springs, WV 25411

Distributed by
www.timrowlandbooks.com

Cover design by Ryan Harpster, Silverback Designs

ISBN 978-0-9761597-3-5

Dedicated to...

Hannah, Pete, Nelson, Becky, Cappy, Brooke, Basilio,
Nochero, Copperfield, Sterling, Magellan, Chester,
Tillie, Heidi, Hillary, Nick, Alvin, Doodlebug, Lillie,
Cleopatra, Heifertiti, Princess Beans, Lucy, Hattie, Stink,
Chuckles, Igor, Racer, Nuisance,
and the other chickens who have no names....

and, of course, Opie

Table of Contents

Introduction

Will Rogers said he ever met a man he didn't like; by contrast, my wife Beth and I never met an animal we didn't like. No question about it, our course is less challenging than Mr. R's. But that doesn't mean that our souls have not been tried time and time again, and our patience stretched well beyond the breaking point to the regions where it snaps and sends us over top of Mars.

The animals do not care about this, of course. They exist in a sphere of divine tranquility, and if we have a problem trying to manage or understand them, that's a shame and all, but none of their direct concern.

Although we have dabbled with animals all our lives—Beth is an accomplished equestrian and, growing up in rural West Virginia I did all the requisite 4-H projects that involved the stray pair of pigs and goats—we had confined our respective menageries to pets. Big pets in Beth's case, but pets nonetheless.

It was in the mid-2000s that out paths crossed, and we soon after decided to go for the whole enchilada. We knew we wanted to raise a farm-type animal in some sort of scale, but didn't know which variety would suit. So our small farm soon became something of a stage for tryouts.

We were driven by our love of critters, but beyond that we have harbored growing concerns about the food supply and all the hormone/chemical/antibiotic issues that many readers are probably familiar with and weary of hearing sermons about by now.

We also became disconcerted about the conditions of factory farms and the idea that our bacon and eggs were coming courtesy of poor, tortured animals that would never see the sunshine and never know what it was like to play in the warm grass. Our animals would.

But the sad truth is that the nation's meat supply could have come from animals living in alpine meadows filled with wildflowers and wood nymphs serenading them with lutes, and we still would have wanted to raise these critters ourselves. The love of animals came first, and if they happened to fit in with any particular agricultural or political philosophy so much the better.

So we started with a pair of dairy goats. Or maybe it was the flock of chickens. It all starts to run together at this point. Pretty soon we had an ark-like assembly of about every farm animal that comes to mind. People who collect cars go through the same dynamic, I suppose. After a while the frame of logic shifts from "Do we need it?" to "What's one more?"

A few years into the project, visitors to the farm would ask how many animals we had all told, and I would respond with a haunted look and maybe an eye twitch and stammer about how I lost track many hooves ago.

Of course as a humor writer, the animals came in handy on another front. My mantra has always been that the more bad, discouraging and embarrassing things that happen to me, the more material I have for my writing. In Wall Street circles, this paradigm is known as "leveraging."

But I swear, there were times when the beastly transgressions reached the point that I considered a career change to something involving tech. However, with each trial, with each tribulation, I studiously put fingers to keyboard and recorded it both as vocation and as therapy.

So with this collection of essays, I am letting animals past and present know that I forgive them. I absolve them of their sins, because hopefully some good has come from it, and I can focus on the laughs and entertainment they have provided to both myself and, hopefully, the reader.

Now if only the animals can see their way clear to forgive me.

Egyptian royalty takes up residence on farm
June 10, 2008

You can hardly have a farm without cows, can you? Of course not, although it would certainly be less stressful.

At least it's stressful if you get some of those cows that, in my view, are high maintenance, always having to be milked. Or sheltered, or fed, or watered. My job is demanding enough, I don't want my livestock to be the same way.

So I set out to discover the least labor-intensive breed of cattle in existence, and my research led me to the "Belted Galloway," one of a number of interesting heritage breeds that are outside of the Angus/ Holstein mainstream. They are commonly black with a white band around the midsection and, our friends say, rather resemble a four-legged Oreo cookie.

It so happened that Doug May, a farmer who lives just up the road from us, had a herd and was looking to sell a few. We wanted a couple of young animals, so Doug was kind enough to round up all eligible critters and hold them in the barn for our inspection.

Beth and I each picked out a heifer, and our selection says a lot about the difference between men and women. I picked the biggest and baddest of the bunch, while Beth chose the smallest and saddest.

We named the bigger one Cleopatra and the smaller one Nefertiti (and for the record, I wish to assure Michelle Milken that these names are not indicative of some Middle Eastern terrorist plot on our part).

I have put out a feeler that perhaps we could change Nefertiti's name to Heifertiti, but at this point in time the idea is lacking traction.

The Galloways are low maintenance because they have been bred through the years to survive in the harsh, scrubby highlands of Scotland. In other words, they can eat just about anything that grows, regardless of nutritional value.

We kept them in a holding pen the first evening, where they drew quite a bit of attention from the other animals. The bouvier des Flandres named Opie is used to us bringing home new wildlife, but was completely unprepared for the sheer size of the new additions. He came bounding out of the house to play with the little goats, oblivious for the moment of the monsters that lurked a few feet to the east.

In mid-stride they caught his eye, and there was a discernible "WHOA!" moment as he tried to grasp the significance of these creatures that were five to 10 times his size. "Bouvier" means cattle dog, so buried somewhere in Opie's instincts, one would think, is an index card dictating proper interaction. You could almost see him mentally flipping through the files: "Cattle, cattle; see 'herd.'"

His default response is to give chase, but these cows weren't going anywhere; they just stared back at the dog, enormously unimpressed.

The only beasts that do bother the cows on occasion are the donkeys, who might be playing or might be plotting a kill, it's hard to tell. It's almost exactly like "F-Troop." I'll see Cleopatra and Nefertiti ambling through the field, while high up on the ridge, stalking the cowvalry, I can see what look like four Indian feathers. These feathers, I know, are actually ears, and are attached to two Very Bad Donkeys just out of sight over the brow of the hill.

Nothing much ever happens, largely, I suspect, because the cows easily outweigh anything else on the place. On a farm, size matters.

Dog gone it, daily grind got the best of me
June 19, 2008

Beth and I were driving past Beer Belly Lane in Sandy Hook on Saturday while listening to NPR (I am aware of the incongruity) when the radio-show host started talking about something common in most every dog owner's experience.

This is the propensity of a dog to create an irrational spite against some mechanical device, often a vacuum cleaner, and express this dissatisfaction through maniacal barking.

The radio reception wasn't great, but if I understood correctly, the cure for this is to discipline not the dog, but the vacuum cleaner.

To wit, speak sternly to the vacuum cleaner and show the dog that you are in control of the situation. Demonstrate that you are on to the vacuum cleaner's tricks, and you will in no way permit illegalities by a household appliance.

I gather this is of comfort to the dog, who might fear that the vacuum cleaner is trying to attack you or is in some way a threat to health and home in general.

This assigns a lot of logic to the thought patterns of a dog, an enterprise that to my knowledge has made no person rich. But I was willing to hear the man out.

Far as I know, the bouvier des Flandres named Opie does not have it in for vacuums - I've never used one in his presence, or anyone else's, for that matter.

This is a dog who is not afraid of anything, a dog who thinks everything and everyone is just great. Opie loves the world. With one exception - the coffee grinder.

Every night when I grind the beans for the morning brew, he goes ape—howling, whining, barking, crying—and scampers with agitation around the kitchen, banging into things and knocking over anything that isn't bolted to the floor.

Scolding doesn't work. Letting him sniff the grinder doesn't work. Holding him by the collar and making him sit doesn't work. Counseling doesn't work.

I hit the button and he goes berserk.

It can't be the size; the gizmo is 6 inches high and 3 inches wide. It can't be the noise; Opie will lie right next to the circular saw when I'm buzzing 2-by-4s. I was desperate for ideas, so when I got home that night—well, let's just say I'm glad there's no videotape of what happened.

When he heard the rustle of the coffee bag, Opie was in the kitchen, and he grew more and more restless as I loaded the beans. Then, I employed the strategy.

Timidly at first, I looked at the machine and said, "bad coffee grinder." Then louder, "BAD BAD coffee grinder."

I have to admit, this knocked Opie off his stride. Instead of barking, he cocked his head. So I decided to go for the whole enchilada.

I flipped the switch and as the motor kicked in, I began slapping it and yelling at it, "Lousy, nasty, EVIL, coffee grinder. I HATE you. You are more obnoxious than NANCY GRACE! You PATHETIC, despicable, COMMUNIST coffee grinder."

I got into it. I grabbed the machine and shook it. I yelled, cursed the coffee grinder's ancestors and smacked it across the lid. I told the filthy coffee grinder it was not the boss of me. I violently took the cord and at this point, I turned to see the dog's reaction.

Opie wasn't there. Beth was.

I'm going to stop writing now.

Water water everywhere and some charge $40 a bottle for it
July 1, 2008

At any given time, I generally have a couple of one-liter soda bottles in my refrigerator filled with tap water.

I'm thinking of putting them on eBay.

I might never have considered that they had any value outside of Death Valley, had I not read a lengthy story in the Washington Post this week about water that sells for up to $40 a bottle—despite the contention of experts who were quoted as saying that the main difference between bottled water and tap water is the marketing. Blind taste tests routinely show that no one can tell the difference between bottled water and water straight from the tap.

I was thinking that if I ever had an extra $40 lying around I'd spend it on a gallon of gasoline, but that was before I visited the Web site of

Bling H20, home of the "Limited Edition Bling H2O baby Crimson Red 375ml Bottle, Red Swarovski Crysta."

I have no idea what any of that means, but all of a sudden the idea of drinking tap water out of a Pepsi bottle makes me feel as if I might as well be licking dew off of a turtle.

And certainly I want to be like one of the beautiful celebrity-type people with vacant stares that they show drinking their product. I'm curious though—what makes water a "limited edition?" Do they know something I don't? It's like breathing limited-edition air—makes you think we might run out sometime soon.

You have to admire Bling. It's all about the price. And the bottle —frosted glass, with a cork. They don't even bother trying to tell you that it comes from some secret spring in the Caucuses guarded by an order of blind monks.

I've always been dubious of that angle. How do I know what cattle have been walking through that spring? It's the same way I won't drink any water that has the words "ice" or "glacier" on the label. I don't know where that glacier's been.

It's kind of like Coors wanting you to buy its beer because it's somehow colder than the competition.

The Post story goes on to mention the extravagances of other waters purchased by people who are easily separated from their money —restaurants that serve water for $5 and provide a water steward to ensure the proper water is matched to your food.

And from Hawaii comes a 2-ounce bottle of "concentrated water" for $33.50, which you make into drinking water by, you guessed it, adding water.

You wonder whether people who engage in these practices feel even remotely foolish at some level, or whether they totally buy in.

Personally, I prefer the other end of the scale, one represented by our pig Magellan, who drinks water while standing in it. It should be mentioned that the animal's feet are not terribly clean.

For a while, I kept running him clean water every time he'd befoul the fresh stuff—which was every time he drank. His snout isn't terribly clean, either. I finally have given up on the process as hopeless, when I noticed him in the corner of his pen comfortably munching on a hunk of mud.

To him, water is water and so what if it's brown? In this way, the pig is smarter than the celebrities.

Bear with me while I muse on our recent ursine sighting
July 3, 2008

So what was a bear doing at the Williamsport Sheetz? They come up with a new breakfast sandwich called the shmal- mon? Was he after a scratch-off? And for that matter, what was he doing in Williamsport in the first place?

Maybe he was just passing through on his way to Halfway, so he could go shopping at Valley Maul. (Oh, be quiet; if I have to do a whole column on bear jokes, there are bound to be some weak links, OK?)

According to a story by Herald-Mail staff writer Erin Julius (who refuses to let me refer to her as a Cub Reporter), police began receiving calls early Monday and, for the next couple of hours, the bear led authorities on a wild Pooh chase through the streets of Williamsport before he finally disappeared into the woods.

If you're a lawman, this is about the time you regret not taking the job in Montgomery Village, where the only claws you're ever going to see are on a soccer mom whose kid just got called for tripping. Or whatever it is that soccer kids get called for.

There's nothing dignified about sprinting down the street in full uniform and hard shoes in pursuit of a wild animal. Yeah, you got a shotgun, but even the bear knows you're not going to use it, not when everybody in America packs a video camera. No one wants to be known across YouTube as the officer who blew away Yogi.

18

And thank goodness no one caught it. We don't want another Bucky the Deer situation on our hands.

One very clever officer finally lured the bear with a glazed doughnut, which had to be a tough decision for him (the lawman, not the bear). On one hand, you want to get the bear off the streets; on the other, you risk reigniting the cop-doughnut jokes. You know, like, "You sure it was the cop that lured the bear with the doughnut and not the other way around?"

It also sets a dangerous precedent. If bears get a taste for doughnuts, no morning police roll call will be safe.

Anyway, when the sheriff's deputies finally caught up to it, the bear said, "Do you know who I am?" and—no, wrong jurisdiction. In fact, the bear dashed into the woods near Williamsport Retirement Village.

Wow. That had to create some excitement at the starin' window. I feel their pain. They're thinking, whew, I finally get to retire and enjoy some peace and tranqui ... AAEEEEIIIII!! Of course by that time, the bear was probably wishing he could retire.

Natural Resources folks say the bear—fairly small and about 18 months old—had probably just gotten kicked out of his mom's domain and was looking for new turf he could call home.

First, mad props to the bear community for realizing something that we, as a human race, still haven't mastered. That being, when you turn 18, you need to get out.

There are no 26-year-old bears living in their parents' basements surfing the Internet and showing no real interest in advancing past their career as night manager at Wendy's.

More ominously, however, this young bear has now been rejected twice: First by his mother, now by Williamsport. I hope he has access to good counseling. Rejection is a tough cross to bear.

On the farm, what is good for goose is good for gander
July 15, 2008

I don't write about our three geese much, basically because it would be about as compelling as writing about three cold sores.

They are surly, loud, obnoxious fussbudgets—and those are their attributes. The best you can say about them is that they are fair. They hate everyone and everything equally.

They scream at me when I feed them their corn; they hiss at me when I toss them treats. Their venom is akin to three sour old chain-smoking aunts, always grousing and hacking at the children and wisecracking about their parents.

Matter of fact, I never even bothered to learn their names or sexes, until I needed to for purposes of this column. I had gathered their names were Frankie, Prudence and Edwina. Instead, it's Edwina, Ralphie and Ruthie.

Prudence was Edwina's mother, now passed. Edwina was Edwin until he proved to be a she. I don't know where I got Frankie from. Ruthie is a boy. (Goose-sexing, apparently, is an inexact science.) Beth says I'm free to rename Ruthie by awarding him a more masculine sobriquet. But what would be the point? He is a scruffy, drooling bird who walks with a pronounced limp from some long-ago injury, which only adds to his beauty.

There is absolutely nothing to like about Ralphie—which is why I kind of like him. He's the ringleader of the group, a humorless spokesman for the industry of malcontent, getting in my face and talking smack when I try to be kind and toss him some bread. UPS drivers are all the time asking if the dogs are friendly. I tell them the dogs are fine, but don't turn your back on a goose. Even Opie leaves them alone.

The geese take breakfast at 7 a.m., then exit in a cacophony of displeasure for the creek, where they make life miserable for the mallards, Canada geese, herons and any other wild waterfowl unfortunate enough to cross their ugly paths.

But all that said, they are the spine of the farm. They are the background color on which the rest of the canvas is painted. Their presence is reassuring, because they are consistent—they are always there, squabbling and yakking about some great injustice, but providing comfort by way of their discomfort. If I'm having a bad day, at least I know the geese are having a bad day, too.

They normally drink out of the creek, except when they are too lazy to make the trip, at which point they sip out of the big-animal troughs. Perhaps they did not realize that one of these troughs is now encased by an electric fence that confines the alpacas.

As my good luck would have it, it was Ralphie—the meanest, nastiest goose of the bunch—who made the first move. He tried to maneuver his considerable neck through the electric net when ZAP! After all these years, he finally had something legitimate to complain about. And Ralphie is not a goose to miss an opportunity. He shot across the pasture in three steps exactly. All his past jawing was just for practice; now he broke out into an apocalyptic volcano of goose profanity that probably was heard in Greencastle.

I should have been smug. I should have been happy about seeing this blunderbuss taken down a peg. But there was no joy in it. I felt for the poor guy.

Maybe it was from one gasbag to another, but all I could do was get up from my chair and take him an unelectrified bucket of cold water.

Stripper facing suit comes out of her shell
July 22, 2008

Sometimes it's just a wealth of riches.

On Thursday, we had a stripper getting sued for slapping a customer and the Humane Society spending $130,000 to help box turtles cross the road. Where is one to begin?

Box turtles, obviously. The Humane Society would be proud of me because earlier in the week, I stopped my car to move a turtle out of the road. I did this because box turtle populations have been declining and I believe it is important that we, as a higher, intelligent form of life, recognize our obligation to protect vulnerable species from harm. I also did it because Beth was in the car at the time yelling STTOOOP!

The turtle crossing in question is near Greenbrier State Park, where turtle mortality on the highway had reached unacceptable levels. There was a culvert under the road that turtles could use, but it was small and Humane Society officials were worried that it could cause the turtles to be subjected to poor cell phone service.

The new system will have batter fences that will guide the turtles to bigger, more turtle-friendly culverts. It is interesting that the Humane Society can get a turtle crossing for $130,000 but the government can't put a sewer line under the road for less than $4.5 million.

I'm glad they're doing it. I have a soft spot for turtles, as do all people who were not allowed to have a dog or cat as a child, and for whom a turtle became the Pet of Last Resort. I even went so far as to put a leash on mine to add to the delusion.

And although turtles have their troubles, at least getting a beat down in a strip club apparently isn't one of them. Not so for a fellow who is suing a former dancer at Mitzi's Gentleman's Lounge. The dancer was convicted in a criminal case of striking him across the chops—perhaps the first recorded case of a "slap dance."

It is also historic, in that it is the first strip-club disturbance of the decade not involving Pac Man Jones.

But you're telling me a guy could get slapped in a strip club? No, that doesn't happen, does it? We expect this kind of violence at a Democratic National Convention, but not here.

Dude wants $400,000, half from the club and half from the dancer, who has had a couple of past brushes with the law, including passing bad paper. So good luck with that.

"You want $200,000? Sure, no prob. Do you take checks?"

Maybe she can give him $200,000 worth of provocative gyrations under a strobe light to the tune of Gloria Gaynor's "I Will Survive."

The news story didn't say whether the man in question was married. That would be an awkward decision. On one hand, I have a crack at 400 large, on the other hand I might get cracked in the lemon with an iron skillet—especially if I'd told her I'd been working late at the office that night.

"Uh, honey, good news/bad news. Good news, you can buy that new washer and dryer. Bad news, there's a new cell phone video on YouTube showing me getting a smackdown from a naked chick."

Maybe it's just me, but this might have been one of those times when I just put a bag of ice on my jaw and walk away.

Blondes have more fun—even bulldogs
July 24, 2008

Beth says Hannah the blonde bulldog is not this smart. Well, Hannah may be this smart, Beth allows (she is never one to minimize the animal's qualifications), but certainly Hannah is not this devious.

Opie and I disagree. It's a classic case of the boys versus the girls.

Right off, I admit this is a ticklish situation for me since it involves Hannah (the girl) being the puppet master and Opie (the boy) being the dupe. But I would submit to the court that Opie's young age makes him susceptible to the guiles of an older woman.

It all began when Opie took to making house calls, specifically to the neighbor's house about a quarter-mile down the lane to visit a new Airedale puppy named Katie. He visits other shut-ins as well, including a set of groundhogs who moved away after taking one look at the 100-pound bouvier de Flandres and deciding that they did not wish for a piece of the pie.

And when you're that close to the main road, might as well chase a car or two while you're at it—as many Americans are doing in these days of high gas prices, Opie makes an effort to combine trips.

Needless to say, this type of behavior is Not Allowed, and lands the animal in some pretty serious hot water—including massive scoldings and solitary confinement in the house—with each new infraction.

Hannah has noticed this.

Not that Opie is really in need of a co-conspirator. He's pretty good about lying in the yard and pretending to be asleep—until I turn my back, at which point he goes skulking off down the lane, looking back from time to time to be sure he hasn't been detected.

If he has, he will yawn, stretch and make a casual U-turn before plopping back in his original spot, as if the only thing on his mind was to get the blood circulating a bit.

But increasingly, I noticed him becoming more brazen. He'd wander off, whether I caught him or not, oblivious to my calls. This was odd since he can be disobedient, but is generally not aggressively disobedient.

Then one day I figured it out. The epiphany came as a glint of blonde, maybe 50 feet into the dark woods. Looking closer, I saw, peering out from behind a tree, a ghostly little bulldog face, beckoning like the twin girls in "The Shining."

In dog language, Hannah was calling to Opie: "C-o-m-e ... d-o-w-n ... t-h-e ... l-a-n-e. C-o-m-e ... d-o-w-n ... t-h-e ... l-a-n-e.

In an instant, I had it. Hannah would get Opie's momentum headed in the forbidden direction. Then, while I was in hot pursuit of the boy dog spitting dust and profanity, the girl dog would coolly walk back to the house by another route and feign sleep under a shade tree.

Excitedly, I outlined this new development to Beth: "Don't you see? It's not Opie's fault." For a second, Beth was in a tight spot. To deny my theory would be to diminish her dog's cunning and native wit. But to give the bulldog credit for such skullduggery would open Hannah to criminal proceedings herself.

Finally, she sidestepped the issue: "He should still know better."

Know better? The dog who thinks cabbage is a toy, who thinks alpaca poo is food, who thinks—oh, never mind. There was no point. Boys will be boys, but girls stick together.

Back in the saddle again
July 31, 2008

I'm on painkillers today, so if the column makes more sense than normal, thank the pharmaceutical industry.

The source of this discomfort, and I do not mean to point fingers, is the happy horse Cappuccino, who, in her defense, did not step on me after I hit the ground.

I don't want to say I fell off a horse. That's not heroic enough. Thrown off a horse is better, and bucked off a horse is better still.

Except that Cappy doesn't really buck, at least not in the traditional sense. But her mind does tend to wander at times and she will misstep —which normally is not a problem, except at the time I was practicing riding without stirrups. I don't particularly know why I was practicing riding without stirrups, It's just something that horse riders do.

As a matter of fact, I'm still learning about this whole equine world, which is still rather new to me. For example, when a horse stumbles and the rider goes flying tuchus over teakettle, everyone in the ring goes running over to the horse to make sure it's OK.

Except for Beth, who was more than a little concerned for my well-being.

"Don't try to get up," she said.

No advice was ever less necessary.

After five or 10 minutes I was able to stand again, and I even got back on the animal—which is another horse thing. You have to prove to yourself and others (with emphasis on "others") that a bad fall has not changed your opinion of riding in general. The horse plugged along ably enough, with me kind of lolling along on top, vaguely aware that if I fell again I wanted it to be to the right, so the pain would kind of equal out.

The sore ribs and the pie-pan-sized bruise weren't the worst part. Most of the rather ample swelling occurred right at the waist line, and for a man who is dancing right along the upper edge of his "fat jeans" already, several logistical problems emerged. Most obvious, pants that used to fit no longer did. But worse, the extra arm force required to button them set off waves of fire throughout the bruised rib area.

And women think they have problems.

Beth, ever the animal apologist, was quick to point out that this whole affair "wasn't Cappy's fault." I was more inclined to believe that if Cappy would keep her mind on business and was not always looking around like a Park Avenue tourist, she might have a better handle on her footing.

But Beth won't blame an animal, even when she is the victim. When a flying alpaca bopped her in the eye and sent her to the emergency room recently, she would sit down in front of each new medical-type person and immediately say: "Alpacas are the kindest, gentlest animals on earth and they would never do anything like this intentionally."

To which the medical person would invariably reply: "Uh, OK. Now why don't you tell me what hurts."

In fact, her treatments sort of resemble veterinary science. After my fall, she decided to put me on bute (Advil) and "turned me out" to "self regulate." When this didn't work particularly well, it was determined that I should go on "stall rest."

I don't know what all this did, although by the end of it all, I had the oddest craving for some hay.

Hero on a half shell
August 4, 2008

So it would seem that, after decades if not centuries of relative obscurity, the humble box turtle is moving to seize the day and dominate the headlines as never before.

First came the announcement from the national Humane Society (which has no connection to the local Humane Society that rescues dogs and cats) that it would build a $130,000 turtle subway under a county highway.

And now this: A box turtle is being called a hero after leading investigators to a marijuana patch in Rock Creek Park.

The turtle, known as Turtle 72, had been affixed with a radio transmitter by scientists studying the movement of turtles (yeah, well, after figuring out the Antikythera Mechanism, what's left?) near the Maryland/D.C. border.

The turtle's handler would pay her infrequent visits in the 1,754-acre park—maybe to check the condition of the transmitter, maybe to catch up on old times, the news story didn't say—and he just so happened to track her down on July 14 as she stood, as fate would have it, in a small marijuana patch.

Naturally, authorities were notified, and after some surveillance, they caught the "farmer," a kid from Chevy Chase whose previous claim to fame had been as drummer in a winning Montgomery County Battle of the Bands group.

Aside from ridding the region of 10 highly dangerous marijuana plants, two things stand out. First, what are the odds? Poor kid. No way should the stars align to the point that 1. A researcher duct tapes a radio transmitter onto the shell of an Eastern box turtle and, 2. Of all the hundreds of acres in the park the turtle would happen to visit a marijuana patch the size of a desk top and, 3. On the very day, hour and minute that the turtle was standing in the tall grass, the researcher would happen to burst out of the bush to take her pulse?

I've heard of bad luck before, but this is clearly the most disastrous chance occurrence since hanging chad. And if you're a drug trafficker, you would like to think that you had been foiled by some Colomboesque, crime fighting genius, not a plodding reptile with a brain the size of a thumb tack.

But the second standout revelation is even more disturbing: Does this mean Eastern box turtles are doing weed? Those sly devils. Maybe the "chance" wandering to the M. patch wasn't so random after all. So this is their diet. Berries, grubs and a couple of blunts the size of a hot-dog bun.

No wonder so many of them are getting smashed on the highways. They're all strung out on tree. "Oh, wow man, like here comes a car. And like, dude, it's coming real fast. But I still got lots of time to ..." CRUNCH.

They say a turtle carries his home on his back; but no one mentioned that it's a crack house. Maybe the Teenage Mutant Ninja Turtles were normal before becoming full-blown coke freaks.

Of course, we could turn this knowledge to our advantage. They're having trouble eradicating opium poppies in Afghanistan? Turn the box turtles loose. And pretty soon they'll be stopping your car at the border and going through the trunk with a drug-sniffing turtle.

Beth says she saw a turtle in a wild blackberry patch once, his face smeared with purple, staring up at the canes waiting for another to drop. Now we know that the deal was—always hungry with no true concept of time. If that isn't the definition of a turtle burnout, I don't know what is.

Patch makes horse berry upset
August 12, 2008

Whatever I was expecting, this wasn't it. We were bringing our horses home from where they had been boarded on a lovely, sprawling farm in Pleasant Valley, the idea being that we would be able to ride more often if we didn't have to make the 13-mile drive south every time we wanted to saddle up.

I was still mulling over whether "riding more often" was a good thing or a bad thing when it was time for the move.

To the degree that I thought about it at all, I'd reckoned that relocating a couple of horses would be like relocating a couple of cats, only bigger. We'd throw them in the cat carrier/horse trailer, they would sniff their new perimeter, they would be indignant for about 20 minutes and then go to sleep.

I should have known better. Beth, who is Never Wrong in equine matters, had been tense for about a week. She had addressed more contingency plans and questions of "what if" than an Exxon executive contemplating an Obama presidency.

Horses are different from other animals, in that their management is 3 percent science and 97 percent superstition. Nothing is simple or predictable.

Loading a horse onto a trailer (particularly if it is not used to trailers) is something everyone should try once, but no more often. Sometimes you can lead the animal right up and in. If that doesn't work, you tempt it with a carrot while tapping on its rear hocks with a riding crop. If that doesn't work, you string a long, nylon strap around its hindquarters and pull, inch by inch. If that doesn't work, you get down on your knees, draw a chalk circle on the pavement, place three stones in the circle, sacrifice a goat and begin to chant.

Fortunately, we got Beth's mare Brooke in using Step 3. My horse, Cappuccino, is a big girl—half draft horse, half thoroughbred—who likes to eat, so one whiff of a carrot did the trick.

But once we got home, it was Cappy's turn to freak. I never knew much about mares before, but to them, everything is High Drama. For drama, mares make a teenage girl look like Alan Greenspan. When we tried to lead them to their new paddock, Cappy went absolutely nuts over—a strawberry patch.

Yes, a strawberry patch. Beth said Cappy may not have liked the red color. Keep in mind, this is a farmette with cows, donkeys, goats, chickens, dogs, a pig ... all manner of distractions you might expect to spark an anxiety attack in a nervous animal. Cappy paid none of these any mind. But for some reason, she believed the strawberries were out to kill her.

Beth is always telling me these weird rules about horses: All dogs bite, all horses kick. (Even horses that don't kick are just patient—they will wait 20 years waiting for that one clear shot.) Do not get scared around a horse, because the horse will feed off of your feelings. And never, ever wrap the lead rope around your hand.

This is because that when an animal that outweighs you by 1,100 pounds decides that it wants to go, it will go, and if your hand—and nothing else—comes along for the ride, that is not the animal's concern.

For Cappy, the strawberries were not a reason for being, they were a reason for going. Long story short, Beth's advice probably saved me a few fingers. It took her about a hundred yards before she was assured that the strawberries were not following her.

But all's well that ends well, and for me it was a good lesson learned. Next year, I'm planting June berries, not ever-bearers.

Magellan the pig as adventurous as namesake
August 21, 2008

You might be surprised at the number of people who ask me what it's like to own a pet pig.

Actually, that number is zero, but this does not matter because I am going to tell you, regardless of the general public's apathy concerning the topic.

Magellan has been in the Little Farm by the Creek family for about three months now, so I have had the chance to form some opinions. So has he.

This is not some exotic, pot-bellied pig. He's just a plain old hog. He escaped the traditional hog fate because of his smaller stature and because the McCormick family from whence he came said—and maybe I should have "read between the lines" on this one before taking charge of him—that he had something of a "unique personality."

Does chasing riding lawnmowers for sport constitute a unique personality? You tell me.

I said Magellan is small, but that's relative. I'd say he's about 200 pounds, and if he wants to go left there is nothing short of a front-end loader than can make him go right. I built him what I considered to be a rather substantial residence, but for amusement he moves it around his lot like a doll house.

Believe it or not, he's also fast and athletic. If he's not the smartest animal on the place, he's in the running. He loves people; he loves the other animals. He's always in a good mood. He sees us coming, he comes running, wagging his curly little tail like a dog.

In fact, Magellan blows away just about every stereotype you might have about pigdom. Now, if it just weren't for those dicey personal habits, which have caused me to enact a couple of hard-and-fast rules:

1. Never feed Magellan wearing light-colored clothing.

The animal loves to nuzzle, which is nice in a pet, unless it's plastered in a full half-inch of caked mud and dirt. He's also, where food is concerned, not a particularly patient pig. On the upside, he's a zucchini-eating machine. In this respect, he is a lot more courteous than are many friends and neighbors who lock their doors when they see you coming with an armload of the product.

2. Forget about "physical improvements" to a hog pen.

Any time I try to make a change in his surroundings he takes the ball and runs with it. This is problematic, considering that he is an animal who can pull nails with his teeth. I tried to shovel out a level spot for his water tub. He took this as a "starter kit" and in 20 minutes there was a moon-sized crater where a hydration unit had once resided.

It is, of course, no matter to him. Given the choice between drinking out of a clean tub and a mud hole, he'll take the mud hole. For him, water is not properly flavored unless it is the color of chocolate milk.

3. DO NOT get him wound up. He is an excitable pig, and when you mix a quagmire of mud and manure with 200 pounds of happy pork, the results are not pleasant.

It should be said that Beth does not follow this rule. When she's mowing the paddocks, she has a habit of calling out and egging on the ham. Magellan is just ecstatic over the attention and bounds around like an overinflated race horse. We have an electric wire around his pen, but he gets so excited that when they touch, he shocks the fence.

All this energy even makes Opie nervous. But Beth wants to put a harness and leash on Magellan and walk him around the farm. I say, good luck with that. If you see a pig sprinting through the county with a woman flying behind like a parasailer, you will know the experiment was a failure.

Horse act is a neigh-win situation in family barn
August 28, 2008

There's a sign at a church outside Boonsboro that reads, "Horse Sense is Stable Thinking."

I hadn't thought of the phrase "horse sense" in a long time, and my dealings with horses over the past year had done nothing to jog my memory.

Horse lunacy. Horse freakout. Horse neuroticism. Horse from a planet that is very different from ours. Those have all popped into my head. But horse sense? Not so much.

Except there is this:

Horses, Beth says, have learned how to get through the day by doing the bare minimum necessary for existence. (In the days before they righted the ship, you could have expected a Division of Motor Vehicles joke here, but sadly that is no longer the low-hanging fruit that it used to be.)

Outside of that, my only thought was that someone coined the phrase "horse sense" sarcastically, but somehow the meaning got lost in the translation.

Cappy and Brooke have been with us for about two weeks, and for a while they were a two-mare support group, clinging together like equine Velcro as they attempted to get a handle on their new surroundings.

After about 10 days, however, they both happened to remember this fundamental truth: They hate each other.

I don't quite understand it, but Beth says it's because each is determined to be the Head Boss Mare of the Universe. She says that mares, not stallions, set the rules (horses are like people in more ways than I thought) and when you have two mares with strong opinions of themselves it can lead to tension, tension being defined as bared teeth, ugly faces, pinned ears, stomping and vicious kicks.

We had installed a fancy and expensive steel-bar divider between their stalls so they could see each other. Now we're going to have to cover it with plywood so they can't see each other.

And if one of them is in season? "Twelve hundred pounds of PMS," Beth says.

They have these flare-ups a couple of times a day, then they go back to being fast friends.

Cappy is the more laid back of the two, although if provoked, she will not back down. Fortunately, she can be bought. Had Cappy been Emperor of Japan in 1931, she would have called back her troops massed at the Manchurian boarder if Secretary Stimson simply offered her a carrot.

In the middle of a fight, Cappy will suddenly realize she's hungry and begin to graze. This infuriates Brooke all the more—until she realizes that the grass does look pretty good and they spend the next six hours placidly munching, nose to nose.

Anyway, to head off any perceived slights, we have to maintain a strict regimen: Brooke gets to leave the barn first, Cappy gets to enter the pasture first, Brooke gets a drink of water first, Cappy gets her carrots first. ...

One of these days, we hope to actually get to ride them, instead of having to continually be renegotiating Yalta. It's discouraging that on a peaceful farm, I now find myself in the exact same situation that I used to find myself in my younger, more urban days: Trying to understand women.

Farmers must be psychologists to weather storms
September 11, 2008

One senses that if it were up to Magellan the pig, he'd order up a hurricane every day of the week.

It's interesting to see how different animals cope with six hours of driving rain in different ways, and Magellan was clearly the most comfortable with it of any critter on the farm.

He greeted the soaking the way an unemployed Key Wester greets a sunny day on the beach. He parked himself right out in the open and went to sleep, the only movement coming from his sides as he breathed out a particularly contented grunt.

He was on a bit of a slope, and after a bit, the rivulets of water began eroding the mud on all sides of him, leaving him sound asleep on a pig-shaped pedestal as the ground around him washed away.

Hurricane Hanna had another singular effect on the porker: For the first time since we had him, he was clean. As a general thing, he walks around wearing about a wheelbarrow's worth of mud for a coat and so we've never had an accurate sense of his true shape and color. Turns out he's a dark red, but he could have been zebra-striped for all we knew.

The bouvier des Flandres named Opie was also pretty much okey-dokey with the storm—basically because his coat is so thick you could run him through a car wash without the moisture ever reaching his skin.

He also thought it was pretty cool that at a full sprint he could leave a 6-foot rooster tail of water in his wake, further soaking any man or beast that happened to be too close. It's doubtful even a tornado would bother Opie, probably because he so closely resembles one himself.

The donkeys and cows stayed out in the rain, but there was a key difference. The cows don't make a big deal of it. They go off and lie down under some out-of-the way tree, occasionally taking a bite of grass to pass the time.

The donkeys, however, never miss the opportunity for drama. They pick a tree that's in plain sight of the house and stare in at us, with the express intent of making sure we can see how miserable they are. Their ears droop, their shoulders slump and they spare no effort in displaying their suffering in a good strong light.

They say that donkeys are biblical, and they are, in the sense that they resemble Job. There's a reason that Eeyore makes Job look like Katie Couric.

The most miserable animal on the place during prolonged storms is Hannah the bulldog, who was not amused in the least by Hanna the Hurricane.

Under the best of circumstances, Hannah is a sort of stocky, stubby, immovable object that cannot be displaced with a water cannon. Yet she must move, however subtly, because she's always under my feet. She's kind of like an ottoman that anticipates where you want to walk and parks itself there.

Whereas a gentle nudge with a toe will send Opie flying out of your way, such incentives are worthless with a bulldog, whose superstructure most resembles the wide, stable stance of a footed bathtub.

So needless to say, getting her to move outdoors into the rain for any reason, however necessary, is problematic. More problematic is getting the passive-aggressive animal to come back in. She stands in the downpour with an awful look on her face—you are the reason she's out in this, so it will be on your conscious as she grows colder and colder, wetter and wetter, and eventually dies.

So, all told, storms can be rather stressing. Farms, it seems, must not only be staffed with farmers, they must be staffed with psychologists.

Bouncing takes a back seat to, well, the back seat

October 21, 2008

It wouldn't be a complete lie to say that Opie was on his best behavior last Saturday. But there is such a slim line between the animal's best behavior and his worst behavior, that it's almost hardly worth making the distinction between the two.

The bouvier des Flanders was the grand marshal for the Washington County Humane Society's Bark in the Park event at Doub's Woods (my request to the school board to ceremonially change the name of Emma K. Doub elementary to Emma K-9 for a day went unanswered).

Getting there was no problem at all. He loves transit. If a car door at our house is accidentally left open for more than a few seconds, we will find Opie sitting in the back seat awaiting taxi service. And he will not leave; he has more patience than Cubs fans and will wait all day in the back seat, if that's what it takes.

He weighs close to 100 pounds, so there is no dragging him out. If he doesn't want to budge, he will remain budgeless for as long as it takes. Nor can he be lured out for treats or any other positive incentive. Conversely, insults and abuse are pointless. To him, there is no such thing as a discouraging word. He thinks "moron" must be human for "greatest dog ever."

So to extract him from the car, there's only one method that will work: I have to get in and drive him somewhere. Anywhere is fine with him. So I drive him two-tenths of a mile to the church and back. He thinks that's great, and will come bounding out of the car as if he's just traveled through the Rockies on the Royal Canadian Pacific Railroad.

Under his own power, however, things are not always as predictable.

Bark in the Park organizers asked if Opie could walk on a leash. I told them the truth. I said, yes, of course he can walk on a leash. He can also walk over a leash, under it, through it—until he is more tangled and hog-tied than Sarah Palin responding to a question on the International Monetary Fund.

As a matter of fact, the only thing he cannot do with a leash is be led around on one, like a normal dog.

So Opie's grand run at the head of the Parade of Dogs was something of a disappointment. Outside of Hannah, he doesn't see other dogs much, so he wasted no time trying to introduce himself to every other creature on the path. And by "introduce," I mean "wrestle."

And by "creature," I do not limit this to the four-footed variety. He's just as happy to give any man, woman or child a full, leaping bear hug, just to show his love. People who weigh 140 pounds or so can usually handle the impact, but more diminutive folk usually are sent flying into the nearest tree. More than once he forced Beth into nervous laughter with her stock apology: "Well, they don't call them 'bouncing bouviers' for nothing."

About our only other recourse would be to tether him to the ground with a number of lines, much like what they use to hold down Underdog in the Macy's Thanksgiving Day Parade.

Fortunately, these were all dog people, so they understood, mostly.

Still, I feared that Opie might be wearing out his welcome sooner rather than later. This called for extreme action on my part. I didn't want to do it, but there was no other choice: I opened the car door.

Sure enough, he bounded right in and stayed there, planted to the rear seat, for the duration of the ceremonies.

But there is no pride, no sense of victory, in taking advantage of a brain so small.

Animal antics less annoying than ads
October 28, 2008

My one and only question about the upcoming presidential election had been this: Is either of the candidates George Bush? No? Great, then I'm happy with the result, come what may.

I had made up my mind; I was in favor of the election.

37

Yet somewhere between the 400,000th Obama television ad and the 300,000th e-mail warning that he is the Antichrist, I sheared a pin. We had to find a retreat where we could, for a long weekend, be untouched by political trespass.

That's how we wound up in New Jersey.

The reasoning was brilliant on my part, if I do say so. The Garden State is solidly blue, so there would be no reason for advertising by either campaign.

And even though nearby Pennsylvania was still somewhat in play, the Philadelphia Phillies' World Series run would drown out all competing noise.

I was correct on both counts. South Jersey seems to be conservative, yet somewhat open to new ideas. So while McCain-Palin signs were in the majority, they were—I am not kidding—colored pink.

Unfortunately, by the time I had all but mastered New Jersey's Rubik's Cube-like highway system, it was time to leave the lovely shore. More unfortunately, the animals had been waiting up for us.

Although we had arranged for pet-sitters, the pets themselves took a dim view of this arrangement and spent the bulk of the weekend plotting revenge:

Juliet: The small Siamese has always made up in noise what she lacks in size. Mostly, this involves the machine-gun, passive-aggressive purr in the eardrum at 5 a.m.

But due to our absence, she judged that we had to be punished in new and creative ways. Basically, this involved prying a wooden knob off a dresser and batting it around the wooden floor for the better part of the night, punctuated by long pauses and then, just as you're thinking it's safe to go back to sleep, a resumption of said activity.

Waterboarding must feel like a back rub after this technique. It was worse when she stopped the clatter, because all there was to do then was lie there in a state of high tension, waiting to see if the nightmare was indeed over or if this was just a tease.

Hannah: Part of a planned tag team perhaps, the bulldog—she with a face out of "Slingblade" and a shape out of "Free Willy"—took up the cause when the cat finally tailed off.

In the middle of the night, she conceived of an itch in a spot where, given stubby legs and general roundness, no bulldog paw could ever reach.

This led to an hour of huffing, puffing and groaning as she attempted to find a position that would allow claw access to the affected spot. Every so often she would twist herself enough to get close, but just as she did, gravity would take over and she would thud noisily onto her back, with the resulting whoof of air exiting the misshapen nasal passages echoing throughout the room. She is lucky she is so lovable.

Opie: The bouvier des Flanders lacks the subtlety of his roommates and is not contrived enough to concoct a cover story (scratching or playing) for acting out. His approach was pretty straightforward. While we were away, he ate one of those "indestructible" cheeseburger squeaky toys and proceeded to spend the next 48 hours throwing up all over the house.

So we—and by "we" I mean "Beth"—spent considerable time mopping up shards of brightly colored plastic dripping in a sticky and unspeakably fragrant goo.

Which, when it comes down to it, was less repulsive than being subjected to a weekend of political ads.

Thankfully, animals are easy to please
November 26, 2008

In the grand scheme of things, the question isn't as burning as, say, whether to bail out another multi-national bank. But it's still there: Do you feed the animals anything special on Thanksgiving?

If you have pets, you know what I'm talking about; if you do not, your only question is how long will it be until the men in white coats and butterfly nets come to pick me up.

But here's the deal: Holidays are special, and we feel special and because we are indulging we feel as if our four-legged companions should dine on something special as well.

But there's a problem, and to illustrate I will ask our Bulldog named Hannah to come up on stage. She gets fed twice a day, and the reaction is always the same. "WOW! You're feeding me DOG food! This is GREAT! It's my FAVORITE, how did you know?

She dives into her meals like Greg Louganis, and it is a testament to the sturdiness of the steel in her dog dish that she hasn't eaten right through the bottom of it. So the issue is, we could feed her something special—but what's the point?

It's much the same with the other critters. The alpacas don't—won't—eat anything but hay and alpaca pellets. So that's a lost cause. Magellan the pig is much like Hannah, only times 10. The only thing he won't eat is okra. He is a wise pig.

Beth is of the opinion that horses and such should be treated to a bowl of warm bran mash on special occasions. To me, this sounds more like punishment, but I don't say anything.

The wild card in all this, as he usually is, is the big, black bouvier des Flandres who answers, sometimes, to Opie.

To Opie, food is not a priority. This is very unusual for a dog, I think. Food is OK as far he is concerned, but it takes a back seat to other activities that may present themselves at mealtime, such as barking and entering, grand theft flower pot or creating a nuisance.

At feeding time, both of us need to be in the room; if one or the other is absent, he suspects he may be missing something and won't eat. If we make a sudden move, he won't eat. If there is noise outside, he won't eat. Even low barometric pressure can throw him off.

It's ridiculous. The simple act of throwing some kibble down in front of a dog becomes something more along the lines of communion. It must be silent, the lights must be dim and all distractions must be previously mitigated. We gently set his bowl under his nose and then both of us freeze.

He looks at one of us and then the other to make sure we're not doing anything fun, then if there is no other overt stimuli he might start to pick at his meal. As a general thing, that's about the time the UPS truck will rattle up the driveway, and of course then all bets are off.

Opie does appreciate scrambled eggs, but that doesn't seem very Thanksgivingish. Turkey, stuffing, sweet potatoes, cranberry sauce, scrambled eggs—no.

The dog's problem seems to be that standard food isn't disgusting enough for him. We have at least eight species of farm animals on the place, and Opie savors their leavins' like a connoisseur of fine wine. We routinely catch him thoughtfully swirling a helping of goose poo in his mouth as he tests it for flavor, mouth feel and finish.

Actually, this might explain why he is not hungry come suppertime. I guess children have the same issues. You can't break them of that love for processed foods.

Acorn shortage sends squirrels into a tailspin
December 1, 2008

By now we're all used to the headlines with their doomsday warnings of shortfalls and losses, and declining this and that—but I have to admit, I didn't see this one coming: There's an acorn shortage.

Throughout the region, scientists are mystified by the phenomenon; oak trees that normally produce bushels on bushels of acorns are nutless this year.

The fact that there is an acorn shortage worries me less than the fact that an acorn shortage is news. Are things really that bad? Is there a fear that the economy is so shot that we are all on the brink of returning to our hunter-gatherer roots, and an acorn shortage could mean that we will all starve?

I know a little about supply and demand, so if you have acorn futures in the 401(k)—and the "k" stands for kaput—this is excellent news. But short of that, who cares?

It could be this is important because we're only two bank failures from being forced into a mast-based economy.

"Hey, you got change for a walnut?"

"Yeah, two almonds and a chinquapin."

But the importance of the matter, in our "How does this affect me?" society, seems to be the effect the acorn shortage is having on squirrels.

Without their normal foodstuff, squirrels are on the rampage, according to a story in The Washington Post. Calls have come in to animal control offices reporting "crazy squirrels" that are "eating garbage, inhaling bird feed (and) greedily demolishing pumpkins."

Great. As if we didn't have enough problems without this.

In my experience, squirrels have never been particularly shy. And now that they're starving, we have the prospect of the emboldened rodents breaking into the house and raiding the fridge. I can handle a squirrel eating the occasional garden vegetable, but when they come knocking on the door asking for my recipe for eggplant au gratin, I believe they are taking things too far.

When we visited my in-laws, Bob and Alice Sue, for Thanksgiving in Northern Virginia, we couldn't help but notice what appeared to be a large, round and red growth popping out of a small crotch at the top of a young tree.

On closer inspection, it revealed itself to be an apple that one of these destitute squirrels had lugged into the crown. But an apple is not as storable as a nut, so the animal had to make do as best he could. So if you start seeing watermelons and country hams showing up in the treetops, this is what's going on.

Of course it will only be a matter of time until the alarmists, of which I am one, translate the acorn disappearance into a climatic portent of doom.

"Let's hope it's not something ghastly going on with the natural world," said one naturalist.

Oh, let's hope that it is. It would take our mind off the unemployment rate. Besides, isn't that in the Bible someplace? "And thoust shall knowest it is the end of days when thine acorns driest up from thine mightiest oak and thine squirrels shall freakest out."

Well, maybe not in the Bible proper, but somewhere in the footnotes.

There might be a simple explanation for all of this. With an eye toward self-preservation, tree species produce more nuts during times of stress, such as droughts. Last year was wet, so maybe they just afforded themselves a year off. I'm down with that.

If I can go a year without producing anything of value, who am I to criticize an oak tree?

Please, no elite First Dog for Obama
January 15, 2009

So the Obama family is trying to decide on a dog.

At last, something I am highly qualified to comment on, and my comment is "Don't."

But it might be too late for that, since a puppy was promised to the president-elect's daughters, and while it may be permissible for a politician to break promises to the American people, it is not permissible to break promises to young girls.

So with that in mind, my comment would be to be very, very careful. In fact, this decision will, when all is said and done, be far more consequential than, say, where to distribute TARP funding.

And speaking of TARP, get one. Preferably, one that is large enough to cover the entire kitchen floor, or whatever area the First Beast in likely to inhabit. Newspapers are simply not big enough, trust me. And I'm thinking you will want to save crate-training for members of Congress.

The two finalists breeds the Obamas have in mind are a Portuguese water dog and a labradoodle.

Labradoodle. Just stop it, OK? I don't want to hear of any of these designer breeds cooked up just because they result in a clever name. I don't want to hear about any Pomertriever or Bassetweiler or Cockerpincher or any other compound hound. It just smacks of elitism, and that's not the message you want to send right now.

A Portuguese water dog is OK, I suppose, as long as it doesn't offend the Spaniards. According to the American Kennel Club, the PWD is a seafaring breed, which in a tidal area like Washington could come in handy if you believe these reports of the ice caps melting.

But I'm a little nervous about the dog's characteristics, which are described as "spirited, yet obedient."

I happen to have one of these "spirited yet obedient dogs, and the emphasis is clearly on the spirited, with obedient running a distant second.

The bouvier des Flanders named Opie could be described as "spirited, yet even more spirited." He is so happy and spirited, in fact, that you can't punish him. Shake your finger at him, he licks it. Box him in the ears and he thinks that this is The Most Outstanding Thing that has happened to him all day. Insult and abuse he takes for encouragement and praise.

When you think about it, it's a pretty effective stratagem. At times, I wonder what would happen if someone like Barry Bonds would try this tact. The more you indicted him, the happier he would get.

Pretty soon, you give up trying to punish, because it is just no use.

So I'd be careful of these "spirited" dogs. The other sad thing is that this has broken down into a free-for-all between Portuguese water dog and labradoodle owners, each pushing their own mutt-related agendas. Looking through the political lens, I'm thinking that the Portuguese water dogs probably carry with them more votes (no sense offending the Iberian-American demographic), but labradoodle owners might be bigger campaign contributors.

It's a headache, no doubt. Maybe Obama should have promised a kitten. You never hear feline owners get into a fight over whether the Norwegian Forest Cat is superior to the Maine Coon. Or maybe you do and I just don't travel in those circles—a fact that would make me feel truly blessed.

So in the end, the breed of presidential dog probably doesn't matter all that much. Just be sure it knows the basic commands: Come; sit; stay; and, where this Congress is concerned, veto.

You gotta root for 'dirty beard'

February 16, 2009

Score one for the senior citizens. A 10-year-old Sussex spaniel named Stump won Best in Show at the Westminster Kennel Club Show.

(Be honest. How many of you, when you first heard of the Westminster dog show, thought it was held in Maryland?)

A 10-year-old dog? Isn't that like 70 in people years? This would be like Carol Channing winning Miss America.

Stump. Usually, by the time a dog reaches that age, he has a couple.

I watch the dog show for several reasons. One is to test my theory that the size of the handlers is inversely proportional to the size of the dog. You start in the behemoth, working-group class with the mastiffs and the Great Pyrenees, and the handlers are pretty svelte. But by the time you get down to the toy class, you don't know if the handlers have been training the dogs or eating them.

Like anyone, I have my rooting interests. I don't root for any dog that has a bow on his melon. I don't root for any dog—and I don't care how cute women think they look—with eyes that look similar to those of a 17-year locust. I don't root for any dog whose handler has to bring a hairbrush and a blow dryer into the ring.

I root for dogs that look like dogs. I'm pretty simple that way. As a family matter, I also root for bulldogs and, of course, the bouvier des Flandres. Happily, our own local celebrity bouvier, Sondra and Dave Riser's dog named Demetri, received an award of merit.

As best as I can determine, about the same time, the bouvier des Flandres named Opie had his head buried in the mud digging for some Civil War relic, or something.

Hannah the bulldog is very conscious of her appearance, even though the bone structure of her skull appears to be a prototype for early Star Wars characters. Opie, on the other hand, routinely carries several yards of topsoil in his beard and is the happier for it.

They don't call bouviers "dirty beards" for nothing. Opie is always searching for anything interesting, below ground or above. In the recent rains, he found a rather deep puddle in a low spot in the lawn. He amused himself for a half-hour by pogo-sticking into the air, then watching the pattern of the spray from the resulting splashdown. He thought this was great. He thought the splash was the funniest thing he'd ever seen.

When we saw this, we just slumped our shoulders and trudged to our back porch, where we routinely keep a barbecue grill, a few flower pots and a large stack of towels.

So, when I see the Risers, I have to ask them this question: How do the handlers who show bouviers keep their dogs on the ground? In my experience, gravity does not apply in space and gravity does not apply to bouviers.

An interesting feature of the breed is that they do not need a running start to get off the ground. They just kind of instantly levitate and then fly forward, like a V-22 Osprey. They crash about as often, too.

The bouviers in the show trot around the ring peaceably enough, but Opie spends most of his waking life airborne. True story: We had dinner guests Sunday and Beth had to go through three changes of clothes, the victim of muddy-pawed bouvier launches. Finally, she snapped and chased him through three counties with a tomato stake. This might explain why large-dog owners are so fit.

Weed, pest control as easy as laying eggs
April 8, 2009

This year, I resolve to keep ahead of the flower and vegetable gardens.

Hahahahaha.

No, seriously. I know I say this every year, but every year I get closer to meaning it. I am going to get things in the ground when they need to be in the ground—no more waiting until June to plant the lettuce —and I will react with alacrity to any threat. I will be the Paul Revere of early warning gardening action: One if by bug, two if by weed.

Right now, as the weeds and bugs have yet to make a serious appearance, this seems doable. I look at the vegetable garden, where the only green on a sea of brown mulch is a soldieresque row of purposeful, young spinach plants. And I intend to Keep It That Way.

I am more confident than in years past, because I have 18 ready and able assistants. Two weeks ago, we turned the chickens loose.

The decision was partly practical, partly aesthetic. Farms don't look like farms without a band of hens scratching about. And we have reason to believe the eggs are better if they can range over open pastures, which they never do, of course, since they are far too interested in the flower beds.

They follow us around like 18 feathered groupies, and any place where we disturb the soil they move in and "finish the job." Mostly, they seem to be more interested in insects and weed seeds than they are the main attractions. But if they get too destructive, I seal off the bed with chicken wire.

I confess that this is happening more than I would like, to the point where our little farm is bearing some disturbing resemblance to Guantanamo.

Being a softy, I usually carry a little cracked corn in my pocket, which I toss them from time to time. This will precipitate a scratching frenzy, accompanied by a cacophony of appreciative squawks.

This corn-toss can be used as a tool, since they will tear up any grain-littered ground with amazing efficiency. Needless to say, this is a power that I have to use wisely. Before I figured it out, I scattered corn on the lawn—well, it used to be a lawn.

Now, I don't even bother to till. If there's a garden I want to cultivate, I throw some corn on it and then sit back with an iced tea.

It doesn't all go this well. We have a thoroughbred named Brooke and a thoroughbred cross named Cappy, and these horses can be easily spooked. If one water bucket is out of its normal place it can lead to a stampede. The general reaction is, "Oh my HEAVENS, it's a WATER BUCKET, we may ALL BE KILLED!"

So, one afternoon I'm leading Brooke back into her stall, and all is going well until it turns out there's a chicken in it. The cornered, terrified hen shrieked, flapped and ran/flew in circles, turning the stall into a dust bowl of bedding, feathers and hay, and sending Brooke's mane straight on end. The horse didn't care what my plans were at the moment, she was leaving.

Trying to shoo a chicken and chase down a thoroughbred at the same time is not as simple as it sounds.

So there are drawbacks to the chicken liberation movement, seeing as how they tend to take free range to the extreme.

But I see a bright side. The way they can clear cut a patch of foliage means that weeds may never bother me again. Of course, vegetables and flowers may never bother me again either, but I am willing to take the risk.

If, by this fall, all our gardens are simply neat rectangles of smooth, brown, denuded soil, I will consider it a win.

Essence of bovinity something to chew on
April 27, 2009

In the category of "Now that we know that, what do we do?" scientists announced last week that they have decoded the genome of the common cow.

Maybe this means we can now trace cows back to the days when they lived in caves and drew crude pictures of people on the wall. Maybe it means there is now a future for cows with spinal cord injuries that transcends hamburger. I just don't know.

The journal Science says the feat helps explain "the essence of bovinity."

Really, I didn't think it was all that complicated. Eat grass, chew cud, get slaughtered. There doesn't seem to be a whole lot of essence going on there. Unless we're talking about "marbling," what is there

48

to know? Like we're going to decode the bovine genome and discover that a cow is really a sheep?

Or maybe cows are genetically hard-wired for world domination and we just don't know it yet.

The project took six years, cost $53 million and involved 200 scientists from 25 countries. So basically, decoding a cow genome is as involved as developing the software for Photoshop.

Cows have 22,000 genes, compared to 20,000 in humans, which probably accounts for all those extra stomachs. This shows that genes are capable of overthinking the problem. Come on cows, digestion is not that big a deal.

About 80 percent of cattle genes are identical to human genes, which explains a number of people I can think of, whom space does not allow me to list. But you've seen them, staring at the television like a cow stares at a passing car. It's easy to see how they are only 50 genes or so shy of mooing.

But, thinking ahead here, if we can figure out the genes of a cow, we can figure out the genes of a pig. And armed with this information, we can do some genetic splicing and pretty soon you have an animal that provides us with tenderloin wrapped in bacon. So don't knock science before you see the final results.

I happen to have two cows at the moment, Cleopatra and Heifertiti, whose genetic makeup would likely show that they evolved from the Marx Brothers.

I've told them on countless occasions that nothing is expected of them outside of eating, sleeping and calving. But they won't hear of it. They have—and I don't want to hear any theories of how I am in any way responsible for this—a predisposition for hijinks, and spend much of the day sprinting around the farm, bucking, butting heads, rolling in the dust and sacrificing any notion of traditional bovine dignity.

I blame Opie.

The bouvier (literally, cattle dog) des Flandres has most likely taught the poor cows that it's normal to be insane. Their antics pretty much mirror his. In fact, he might have taught them too well.

Being a herding dog, Opie is programmed to chase anything that moves—sadly for Opie, he is such a big goof that nothing, not even the chickens, is afraid of him, so he has difficulty finding anyone who will engage.

A couple of weeks ago, however, my friend Walter was delivering a round bale, when we saw Opie—who knows something about speed —flying full bore around the barn. Finally, I thought, he found something to chase. Except there was nothing ahead of him.

This was puzzling for a split second, until Heifertiti came into a view, sprinting like a thoroughbred and hot on Opie's heels. The herder was being herded by the very subject he was supposed to herd. The poor dog was not the same for a week.

This would be like a cat being eaten by a mouse, and the damage to his ego was severe.

I don't know what happened; I don't know what went wrong. Probably something that has to do with his genes.

Not a calm and cool experience with Hillary
May 4, 2009

Goats give birth after 140 days, the farm journals say. Goats seldom have any trouble with delivery, the farm journals say. A goat will give you several hours' notice before she has kids, the farm journals say.

That settles it. Next time, I want a goat that reads the farm journals.

Our Toggenburg named Hillary clearly hasn't, but then she's never been much of a goat for following rules, so why break old habits? By the way, if anyone out there has an impending goat/birth situation, my experience is that dogs do not help. I'm just saying, is all.

Hillary was late on her due date, but when she finally got around to it, everything sort of happened all at once. It's not supposed to be that way. There are supposed to be five or six hours worth of "warning signs," including some discharge, gentle murmuring, a quest for solitude, loss of appetite, pawing at the ground, nesting in the bedding and such.

These finer points of birth scheduling were lost on our animal. There was no "Super Bowl Preview Show" in her. I was casually throwing some hay in the late afternoon and couldn't help but notice the girl on the floor, panting, bleating and clearly agitated about something. Then my gaze swept aft and I saw a very tiny hoof in a spot where a hoof has no business being.

If I were any kind of man at all, I just would have passed out then and there and been done with it. As it was, I was endowed with just enough staying power to do the one thing men have the superior ability to do in times of crisis: I ran to get my wife.

I burst into our offices primed to disgorge the news.

Beth was on the phone.

I must have looked like some cartoon character who can't get the words out in the face of calamity, gesturing wildly and spouting out multiple verbal derivatives of the word "ock."

So here's Beth, calmly on the phone, "Yes, we have a shipment of 'Dressage in Harmony' coming from England, but it will probably take a few weeks for it to clear customs, you know how it is with heightened security these ..." and here's me pointing frantically at the barn and saying "kkkkHHHH PPPTTT.

Like talking to the deaf, I exaggerated my lip movement and silently said "goooat."

She nodded and kept up the conversation.

I tried again with the read-my-lips approach. "Ahnoo. Eeyou Dooon't Oonderstaand. GOOOT. NAAOOW."

When we arrived back at the barn, we now saw two hooves. And what appeared to be a nose, all sheathed in ick. I rather casually mentioned "discharge" earlier in the column, but let me tell you something, it—no, never mind, I really don't feel like reliving it.

The problem was that our newborn was a big boy and his head was, well, think Mr. Met. We were calling our mentor Tracy on and off, and Beth came running back and said, "You're going to have to pull when she contracts; I'm going to go call (our farm neighbors) Walter and Tina."

51

Weakly, I said, "Pull? Pull what?" Pull—that? Um. When she contracts what? Really, I don't mind going to make the call."

But by that time Beth had hurried off. I looked at Hillary. Hillary looked at me. I don't think the present circumstance would have been a first-choice situation for either of us. "Yeah Hillary," I said as I put on the surgical gloves, "I didn't think it would ever come to this either, but here we are."

When Beth returned, I had a head out and Beth thankfully did the rest. Which was a good thing, because by then I was shaking so bad I couldn't have delivered a pizza.

The good news is that we have a healthy new addition, Nicholas, to the farm and that I have slightly calmed down. The bad news is that we have another pregnant doe, who is due any minute.

Ill-fitted pair finds short-term love on the farm
May 11, 2009

We've all seen those miserable, cutesy little feature items about dissimilar animal species that hook up to form an unlikely bond—a dog and a cat, a goat and a chicken, James Carville and Mary Matalin.

These spots annoy me as much as the next person, so you can imagine my horror when, on Little Farm by the Creek, a miniature horse and a goose got together and decided that no one was going to out-Walt Disney them.

The affair lasted all of 10 days, then it was over. It was hot and passionate as all forbidden loves are, and as usual, it deeply hurt an innocent bystander. Besides me, I mean.

Anyone familiar with miniature horses knows that what they lack in size they make up in attitude, and such is the case with our Doodlebug, more commonly known as the Little Puke. He escapes at every opportunity, runs away when called, shrieks when dissatisfied about something and harasses any other animal with which he comes in contact. If the world is his oyster, he is the MSX bacteria.

In fact, the only critters on the place that are more ornery are the geese. They hiss, attack and bellow at the top of their lungs. And that's when they're being fed. Any less-fortunate occurrence is greeted with a trebling of the decibel level.

We recently lost one of our three geese, and while we said all the right things about being sad and it was a real shame and all, there was little conviction behind the verbal sympathy cards.

So now we are left with Frankie and Edwina, a bickering old couple that stays together only because of the expense of hiring a divorce attorney. When they're not screaming at someone else, they're screaming at each other (This isn't a home, this is a prison! Well then, get out! I will get out! You wouldn't want to make me that happy ...).

Since they're never pleased with anyone, I never expected the dynamic to change. Then one morning I saw Beth staring at Little Puke's paddock, words escaping her. There was Frankie, grooming the horse with his beak and rubbing his head on its belly. More astonishing, the goose was still alive; this is the type of transgression the L.P. usually addresses with a hoof to the groin.

For the following week, the two were inseparable. Frankie followed Doodlebug into the pasture and the pair would engage in serial nuzzling.

For her part, Edwina would watch from a distance, working herself into a white rage. Frankie would eventually return and try to walk past her as if nothing was happening. Edwina followed on his heels, yakking into his ear at full volume about the scandal of it all. Frankie would just walk faster, but every so often he turned around to give back what he was getting.

The whole scene made me kind of uncomfortable in ways I can't explain.

Of course this couldn't end well. The Little Puke, whose opinion of himself is something along the lines of an equine pope, began to sense that he was seeing someone below his station—like a duke who has a brief fling with the parlor maid. (For clarity, I should mention that Doodlebug has been neutered and geese tend to be gender unspecific, so Frankie might or might not be a boy and Edwina might or might not be a girl. So the lines of sexuality and predictable relationships here are blurred.)

Before long, when Frankie would approach, Doodlebug would gallop away. The goose was crushed—a feeling that couldn't have been helped by Edwina, who took him back with the understanding that she was free to browbeat him through eternity with I-told-you-so's.

So as of this writing, I would tell you that things are back to normal. Except that with geese and miniature horses, they never are.

Price of goats dropping with grip on reality
May 21, 2009

Beth tells prospective customers that our three baby Toggenburg goats "will never be cheaper than they are today." I suspect the reason is because, if we keep them around much longer, we will be so deeply insane that money will be of little comfort.

Every morning at 6, I open the door to their quarters, and a pile of goats falls out on my feet in a tangle of flailing legs, ears and noses, borne of the fact that they have all been leaning heavily against the impediment in wait for their morning bottles.

This noisy goat wad has to be painstakingly untangled before breakfast can commence, but they do not seem to realize that they are contributing to the delay. Once separated, they launch themselves at their bottles with imperfect accuracy—more than once, the collision has sent a stream of warm goat milk straight into my eye which, take it from me, is not the Kellogg's best-to-you-each-morning way to start a new day.

The littlest kid—Abbie—is the biggest pig and the biggest pain. She always finishes first, then proceeds to attack her brother Alvin and cousin Nick, trying to hog an extra gulp or two. Her preferred launch site for the invasion is from the top of my head where she has climbed (while I am still trying to feed Nick) in anticipation of a tactical air strike.

By this time, Alvin has finished and has draped himself around Beth's neck like a mink stole, until he realizes there are hijinks afoot, at which point he happily joins the Nick-Abbie bottle wrestle. Feeding these monsters pretty much leaves us exhausted, at 6:05 a.m.

But the kids are just getting warmed up.

We leave them in their shed while we go milk their mothers, and the noise they make in our absence can best be described as that of a Civil War re-enactment in the middle of a thunderstorm. We can hear multiple crashes and pounding. We do not know what they are doing, and we do not want to know. The revolutions of Europe may have been more productive, but they couldn't have been as loud.

Needless to say, at several points during the day we need to let them out to burn some excess energy. Mainly, they follow me around as I do the chores, which is a bit like having an audience of hyperactive gymnasts doing cartwheels and backflips through your work and destroying any chance of progress.

The happy little elves like to help me clean the horse stalls. The first time went along well enough, until Alvin decided to jump into the muck bucket. After about .02 seconds, he figured out that this was really a place he Did Not Want To Be, so he tried to extract himself post haste. He had landed in the bucket upside down, so he engaged in some goat version of the backstroke.

The result—well, never mind the result, I'll just say that the next time I need to fertilize the pastures, I won't bother with a manure spreader; I'll just fill a big tub up with poo and throw a goat in it.

Struggling mightily, he was halfway out of the bucket when hapless Abbie wandered past. Alvin was struck by a clear case of mission-creep. If he could get out of the bucket AND destroy his sister with the same move, well, that would be about the best day a baby goat could ever have.

And he did it, too. Or was about to, when the goat-missile Nick came flying into the party unannounced, crashing into Alvin, who careened into Abbie, and sending both sprawling—effectively picking up the spare.

This is only a small slice of what goes on all day. There's more, of course. But it is enough to explain why, from the moment they were born, the price of goats has continued to come down.

Healing heifers' hearts
June 1, 2009

The alpacas on our farm were all boys and the cattle on our farm were all girls, a circumstance that has slowed our breeding program considerably. I don't think the species cross, so my dreams of an "alpacow" that would produce steaks, and a sweater to wear while grilling them, never came to much.

So we turned to Doug May, who loaned us a belted galloway bull to come in and do the favors for the heifers Cleopatra and Heifertiti. The bull did not have a name; real ranchers don't name the animals, but we are not real ranchers. Doug was nice enough to tell us, without snickering, that we were free to name the bull if we felt so moved.

Beth wanted to name him Dandee, but I believed that this was not a proper sobriquet for a tough hombre bull stud, so we compromised and called him Dan the Man.

We off-loaded him the day before Mother's Day, appropriately enough. The heifers gave him a quiet stare, but our miniature horse, Doodlebug, was more demonstrative. The Little Puke neighed and whinnied and tossed his mane all about. I think the heifers wanted to be sure that Dan knew they were not interested at the moment. I think Doodlebug wanted to be sure that Dan knew he was a horse.

Dan is young, and not terribly worldly. He got on the wrong side of the creek and couldn't figure out how to get back to the females.

56

His bawling drew disgust from Cleopatra, who just continued to graze with an unspoken resolve that this fellow would not be the father of her children.

But Heifertiti, herself a youngster, took an awkward, Disney-animation-like shine to Dan, and feeling sorry for him, splashed to his side and nudged him down to a shallow crossing. I have several witnesses to this rather unlikely occurrence.

Back at the barn, Dan figured that "she must like me," so he made his move. I had my doubts of his effectiveness. Watching through the window, I told Beth that Dan was mounting Heifertiti.

"Great," she said.

"Not really," I replied.

"Why not?"

"He's mounting her head."

Heifertiti had backed herself firmly into a corner, with her rump planted into the barn wall, limiting Dan's romantic options.

I walked out, put my arm around the bull and told him not to take this the wrong way, but that whoever had taught him about the birds and the bees had been grossly misinformed.

He tried again, pushing her away from the wall, but she began walking in circles, never allowing him a clean shot. The goats, meanwhile, were watching from up on the hill and guffawing their fool heads off. The content of their bleated commentary can only be imagined, but seemed to run along the lines of "Hey Dan, try getting her drunk, har har har."

The two animals continued to circle. Dan's eyes were rolled back in his skull at this point, as he tried to explain that this was a biological need and that everyone back at the farm was doing it and that if she really loved him ...

Beth seems to think that the two kids will figure it out eventually. And for all I know, this was just a cow version of dinner and a movie, but I'm still a bit dubious. All the heifers in the world, and we get the one with the morals of Sister Angelica.

The world ac'cord'ing to a farmer
June 15, 2009

Even part time, pretend farming can be a humbling experience. Whenever I've preserved a flower bed by outsmarting a chicken, I sadly feel as if it's been a good day.

Those days are rare, however. Last week, I needed to mow a pasture, which involved racing a donkey to an open gate. The animal proved faster than the tractor and I spent the rest of the afternoon engaged in donkey chasing, and my initial job never got done.

What should be simple chores become major feats of engineering. Our goat barn has no electricity, so to provide juice for a temporary light, I strung a heavy-duty extension cord from the donkey barn above the cow paddock to the goat barn. I want to emphasize that it was hung using only UL-approved roofing tacks.

When I needed to plug in a circular saw in the milk room, I needed an extra 10 feet of slack in the extension cord. As anyone can see, this is a job that should require all of 30 seconds, provided no animals were present.

Animals were present.

Specifically, two donkeys (Becky and Nelson); five cattle (Cleopatra, Heifertiti, Dan the Man, Porter and House); and two goats (Heidi and Hillary).

Heidi had the first serve. When I reached for the cord, she tackled me. This was accomplished by standing on her hind legs for the space of a few seconds and then coming down full force with her forelegs around my neck. As goat take-downs go, it's pretty effective—and very funny, from her point of view.

When I got back up and looked out the window, I couldn't help but notice Becky across the way calmly chewing on the extension cord, which I had taken down so it could be restrung.

I am not proud if this, but my first instinct was to plug the cord back in and then let the donkey do her worst.

But, being the higher animal, I instead removed the line from her mouth and secured it back out of reach—which meant that I could no longer pull out the necessary slack.

I thought this over for a while. Time passed. It was pretty clear that Becky had all day and was not interested in relocating. So I pulled the cord back down in the donkey barn, pushed a few more feet into the goat barn, pulled it down into the cow paddock and put it back up in the donkey barn.

Check and mate, I thought. I had the donkeys covered. I had the cows covered. I had the goats covered. I did have the goats covered, right? I wouldn't have been so stupid as to—at this point I saw the extension cord moving on its own.

Unlike most animals, goats love anything that's new and different. Throw one in their pen in the morning and they would be one of the few life forms left on the planet to be genuinely interested in newspapers.

So this new cord was exposed to standard goat procedure: Inspect. Rearrange. Destroy. Eat.

In the time it took me to drop everything and sprint to their quarters, the goats had crocheted the cord throughout the slats in the hay mow, which took about 10 minutes to detangle and gave the cattle plenty of time to move in for mop-up duty.

This consisted of trampling the dropped extension cord into about 6 inches of barnyard goo.

At this point—when most men would have taken a seat on a rock and wept—I reached deep down and somehow summoned the resolve to do what I do best.

I gave up.

No one needs to use a circular saw that badly.

Cats live to make people look foolish
July 6, 2009

Editor's note: The cat who is the subject of this column was retrieved Monday from the tree in which it had been lingering since June 29.

So cut down the tree already.

As of this writing, Washington County's long national nightmare was entering its seventh day, as we all wait breathlessly to find out what will happen to a cat that has been up a tree since June 29. It's like Ted Koppel and the hostages in Iran. Day 285, nothing has changed.

It has been a slow news week here in Hagerstown, I take it, since the public has been hanging on every word written about the stubborn feline while paying scant attention to more memorable area events, such as the Mile-Long Plus Yard Sale on Longmeow Road. Longmeadow Road. Sorry. You see how mesmerizing a cat story can be.

Even The Herald-Mail's best efforts to drum up interest in other local events (actual Monday headline: "Excitement building for Ag Expo and Fair") have done little to distract readers from their paws célebré.

OK, first things first: Cat, if you're listening, you darn well better not come down before this column is published, and if you do, you had better come down alive. I don't want to wake up this morning to front page photos of a kitty pancaked on a driveway—or worse, a chalk outline—which will make me look like a heartless jerk for making light of the situation.

Second, I officially support the Humane Society, which has adopted the Little Bo Peep strategy (leave them alone and they'll come home) in cat-retrieval methodology.

Phone rings down at the Humane Society and, every time, they have to pray it's not one of these situations. Like, what are they supposed to do? We all know what happens when you try to get a cat out of a tree: It climbs higher. And that's what happened here. Well, God

60

and the Washington County Humane Society cannot help people or cats that are unwilling to help themselves.

Not much is known about this particular cat. Maybe it's like those pole sitters, who are always shooting for a Guinness record. Maybe its a member of a religious cult, the Branch Dikittyians, who believe that when you die, your soul goes up in a tree and won't come down.

So many questions: What's her name? Isn't she hungry? Thirsty? What is she using for a cat box? Related question: Is it safe to stand under the tree? What kind of tree is it, a purrsimmon?

Poor cat. I know what it's going through because our cat Juliet will occasionally climb up a walnut tree and then compound the problem by leaping over to the roof of the old smokehouse, reasons unknown. There she discovers, for she never remembers, that tin roofs provide poor traction.

When she tries to dismount, she starts to slip, so she whirls around and makes for the peak of the roof, all four legs windmilling like Scooby-Doo getting away from a spook. Back atop, she howls as if being stuck with knitting needles, in a tone that is distinctly accusatory, as if the whole indignity is somehow our fault. This sets up one of those regrettable "people talking to animals as if they will understand" scenarios. "YOU got yourself up there, so YOU figure out how you're going to get down. Don't look to ME to clean up YOUR mess. You hear me?"

Eventually though, I climb a ladder to the base of the roof and spread my arms for the catch. Juliet looks down at me and thinks it through. Time passes. This is a solution neither of us wants.

But eventually, she will let go and do that sliding board thing into my arms, the force of her sudden arrival knocking us both off the ladder and down onto the ground as a general thing.

The lingering question in these things is whether the cat was worth saving in the first place.

Broody duty has disastrous underpinnings
July 8, 2009

If you have ever raised chickens, you probably know about something called a "broody hen." If, however, you have never raised chickens, can we arrange for a brain transplant so I will have no memory of ever having done so?

Broody hens are basically chickens that want to become mothers. They stop laying eggs and do nothing but sit sullenly on a nest all day watching "The Guiding Light."

Since we do not have a rooster, the eggs they sit on have no chance of hatching, but the chickens do not know this. Chickens, as a general thing, do not know much of anything outside of food consumption. They are like earthbound seagulls, flocking to any other animal that is being fed in the hopes of snagging a few leavins'.

Five of our hens went broody all at once, which seriously ate into our egg production. This nonsense had to be stopped, but unbroodying a hen is like trying to smarten up a national banking executive.

As usual, we read all the books. As usual, they didn't help. The book says to confine the hen in a cage and hang it from the ceiling where the breeze will "cool off their torrid underpinnings." I can photocopy the page and send it to you if you think I am lying about this.

Aware that there can be nothing more dangerous than a female with torrid underpinnings, I took the work seriously. But I'll be darned if I were going to hang up five chickens in cages like they were parrots or something, on the chance that a visitor might think I was part of some freakish religious cult.

We researched further, and Beth found a post from an old British countrywoman who swore that if you "dipped the chicken's bum" in a bucket of cold water, it would immediately cure the problem.

I let this info process in the old melon for a bit.

Sensing my skepticism, Beth said, "It sounds weird, but I bet it works; those Brits don't put up with any foolishness."

"Yeah, well, two words: Monty Python. How do we know this isn't one of those bizarre stunts they pass off as humor, like camel spotting or Twit of the Year competitions?"

But desperate times call for desperate measures. I did two things. I put the bucket in a corner of the barnyard where no one could possibly see me. Boonsboro is a small town and people talk.

Second, I explained to the chicken that this wasn't my idea, but she had better cooperate anyway, or the next time she entered water it would be boiling, with carrots and a bay leaf for company.

The first two hens took it reasonably well, but the third chicken Did Not. Her underpinnings had just gone from torrid down to sweltering when she went on the offensive. I'd been careful to make sure that I had her wings pinned to her sides, but not careful enough, apparently.

For a real, live approximation of what happened next, just put a down comforter into a swimming pool and slice through it with a chainsaw. It was like when Dorothy threw water on the Wicked Witch, although more dramatic.

But did it work? I don't know; I couldn't go near the chicken coop for about three days. Beth said it seemed to work on three of the five, but from now on they can just go broody for all I care.

For me, there will be no more chicken baptisms. You can bet your underpinnings on that.

Pants on the trees keep water in the trough
August 3, 2009

In my defense, I'd been on the road for a few days in several hotel bathrooms. Maybe that's why I found myself staring at my own home shower controls, trying to remember how to shut the water off.

I have less of an excuse for what happened the next morning.

Beth always leaves my lunch on the same table where we dry our goat-milking supplies after they've been sanitized. So on my way out the door, I picked up the milk funnel and started taking it to work instead of my lunch.

Fortunately, Beth was there to administer a gentle "ahem" before I got too far.

The "ahem moments" are getting more common and my mom tells me it will only get worse. I like to think it's because I have so many other critically important issues on my mind that I can't be expected to remember the small stuff.

But when your chief job requirement is finding a word that rhymes with "booger," that's a hard case to argue.

A couple of weeks ago, I was in a hurry to get something or other, and I purposefully strode into Cappy's stall and then—just stood there. The big horse looked at me like, "Yes?"

I slunk out of the stall, trying to figure out what I'd been after in the first place and why I thought I might have found it in a bare stall.

Cappy did her best to wave it off, but the moment was clearly awkward. When a horse feels embarrassed for you, something's seriously amiss.

Between us, Beth and I like to say that we have one good memory, but even that would be an optimistic assessment. We have several, hundred-gallon troughs used to water various critters. They must be filled with a hose, which takes about 15 to 20 minutes.

Obviously, you can't just stand there the whole time, so we go off and do other chores and come back later to shut off the water. Sometimes much later. I'm talking hours and hours.

We have flooded the entire cattle shed after forgetting to turn off the hose. We have nightmares about it. We wake up in the middle of the night screaming "THE WATER!" before realizing, hoping, it was just a dream.

I had just about come to the conclusion I was entirely untrustworthy on the matter, and from now on would have to stand at the trough until it was full.

So there I was at the horse trough, waiting impatiently, as the water level rose a centimeter at a time. It was only about 6 inches deep when I was struck with the most brilliant idea of my life.

How could I be sure to remember to come back and shut off the hose? Easy. With an air of mental superiority, I calmly took off my pants, hung them in a nearby pecan tree, and smugly turned and walked away.

Maybe Samuel Morse was just as pleased with himself when he invented the light bulb as I was at that moment, but it would be hard to imagine.

Never had the remaining chores seemed so easy and carefree. I mucked stalls, collected eggs and threw hay, all with, as Mark Twain said, "the calm confidence of a Christian holding four aces."

At one point, Beth came out and glanced at me, but didn't say anything. By now, she's pretty much used to bizarre behavior on my part, behavior that makes sense only to me, and has given up trying to figure it all out.

As the sun set, we tidied up the last of the day's work and started strolling back to the house. Finally she couldn't contain herself anymore: "Why have you been so happy all afternoon and why aren't you wearing any pants?"

I tilted my head back slightly and smiled, ready to be showered with her praises of my genius and said, "I am not wearing any pants, because ... because ... THE WATER!"

Opie has yet to find niche
August 5, 2009

Beth likes to say that every animal on the farm needs a job, on the theory that they are happier when their minds are occupied.

So they all have their assignments, although sometimes it requires stretching the definition of the word "job" to the red line.

For example, the donkeys' job is to protect other animals from coyotes. They do this job very well, in the sense that they also—based on results—protect the other animals from wolves, jackals, hyenas, pirates and T-rexs.

We haven't had an elephant attack in years, and all the credit goes to Becky and Nelson.

Some of the critters' jobs are obvious—milk goats, meat goats, cattle, horses and chickens. Others are less so, but still important: Magellan the pig is in charge of our surplus zucchini problem. The boy goats tackle the brush. Hannah the bulldog handles security and every so often a mouse will run into the jaws of the snoring cat Juliet.

This leaves the bouncing bouvier des Flandres named Opie, whose main contribution to society has yet to be identified. At 2 years old, he's still something of a puppy in search of a vocation. (Making the lives of everyone else miserable by way of irrational exuberance doesn't count.)

In fairness to the animal, he's been bred as a herding dog and it's not his fault that nothing on the farm really needs to be herded. But if the cast of "Red River" ever shows up on our place, we'll have it covered.

Opie also appears to be shooting for the Guinness record of longest continuous amount of time spent with head down a groundhog hole, but if pointless obsessions were jobs, the Birthers would be pulling in 40 grand a week.

It wasn't until I was out picking blackberries that an idea hit me. Beth bakes every berry I can find into fabulous cobblers that are key to my sugar-intensive diet. Forget what the government says, if hummingbirds can live off the stuff, so can I.

The berries are relatively easy to pick, but can be hard to find. I was clawing around the woods in search of another patch, and as usual, Opie was bounding alongside. I remembered hearing that the French use hogs to find truffles, so I reasoned that dogs could be used to find blackberries. What would it take to train Opie to become a berry dog, an hour tops?

I called him over and showed him a piece of fruit. "Opie, this is a blackberry," I said in a loud voice. I don't know why, but when we are imparting an important message to a dog we always talk louder. Forget that his hearing can already detect fire sirens in Winchester.

Opie looked at the blackberry. Then he ate it. I showed him another, holding it out of his reach this time.

OK, he'd seen the berry. Now what? I confess that I'm not the world's greatest animal trainer, so I was unsure what to do next. But I knew I had to show leadership and resolve. "Opie," I said firmly, "Uh —go find more."

He raised his ears. Poor thing. He knew I wanted something, he just didn't know what. "Blackberries! Find blackberries!" And I started jumping up and down saying "blackberries" and he started jumping up and down, so we're both jumping up and down (in sight of the road, mind you) and finally he goes tearing off into the brush. When he came back he was wearing so many briars and twigs and leaves that he resembled one of those camouflaged Army snipers, but he had no blackberries.

Looking back, I don't know why I thought the project might work. I would have had better luck training the blackberries to run and then Opie could have herded them and everyone would have been happy.

When livestock get loose, it's a baaaad situation
August 31, 2009

Other people may think that Animals on the Loose are funny, but not me. On the realities of farming, Washington County Extension Agent Jeff Semler says, "If you have livestock, sooner or later you're going to have deadstock."

And to take it one step further, if you have livestock, sooner or later you're going to have escapedstock.

Believe me, I know.

So I felt for Keedysville farmers Imre and Linda Jarmy when two of their sheep bolted from the grounds of Four States Livestock Auction in Hagerstown and immediately booked tickets for Key West.

You really can't blame the sheep. All animals know about Four States Livestock Auction. In fact, they sit around a campfire at night and shine flashlights on their faces and tell stories about Four States. Yes, maybe you're going to go to a happy new farm where you will stand around in green pastures smelling daisies all day, and then again maybe you ain't.

Four States is a dangerous place for Beth and me to go, and we only do so when we have firmly epoxied our arms to our sides so we can't bid on anything. We are better at the husbandry angle than the business angle, and no farmer ever made money by purchasing every animal for which he feels sorry.

The Jarmys' sheep covered a rather impressive amount of ground after escaping sheriff's deputies' attempts at rounding them up. And no, I'm not going to make a joke about calling in a bail baaandsman, so don't ask.

From experience, I know there are two things that make an officer of the law wish he had chosen a career in reupholstering furniture. One is two women in a fight, and the other is a farm animal on the loose. Frankly, I'm surprised sheriff's deputies didn't try to chase the sheep back across the city line so they would be the Hagerstown Police Department's problem.

You wouldn't think that a big ol' cow or sheep or goat would be that hard to catch, but just try it sometime. Our donkeys, Becky and Nelson, seem to sense those rare occasions—rare in this case being defined as about three times a day—that I leave a gate open, and they're gone. It doesn't matter if they're completely on the far side of the farm while I'm cleaning their barn. If the gate is open, they will materialize at the egress and escape.

I don't mind that. What I do mind is that they always make sure I *know* that they have escaped, just to rub it in my face. I can be in my office writing a column and they will come peek through the window. I can be in the yard reading and they will stand under the bird feeder until I see them.

But, of course, I make one move in their direction and they dash off. Same with the sheep, I'd bet. And forget that old "Leave them alone and they'll come home" malarkey.

If the poet had asked Little Bo Peep herself, she would have said, "Leave them alone and they will trample the neighbor's flower bed and eat $400 worth of prize rose bushes."

The only way we have been able to reclaim runaways is through sugar addiction. We get every animal on the place hooked on sweet feed, so if they do not come back to their paddocks in a timely fashion, they will get the shakes and break out in a sweat.

I wouldn't recommend it, but the same paradigm works for children. Just remember, you didn't hear it here.

The ins and outs of pet ownership
September 9, 2009

Ogden Nash defined a door as something that the dog is always on the wrong side of. Ogden Nash didn't know the half of it.

Look, I've had dogs before, I know they always want to go out and —depending on where they perceive the action to be—sometimes want to come in. But Opie, the bouvier, and Hannah, the bulldog, raise the bar. Juliet, the Siamese cat, is worse than both.

Remember the first time your dog scratched on the door to go out? And you thought it was cute? Oh, he's so smart.

He might be smart, but we're not. When our animals needed to come inside, which they were frequently reluctant to do, we got in the habit of rewarding them with treats. "Come in and get a treat," we'd say.

Opie was sitting hungrily in the kitchen one morning and you could almost see the light bulb go off over his head. He walked over to the door and I dutifully let him out. He stood on the porch for what he reckoned was a dutiful amount of time—which was about six seconds —and then scratched to come back in. And get a treat.

I might as well have taken the dog do obedience school and taught him to chew my arms off. Dogs might be fast learners, but they are slow dislearners. Even though we have abandoned the practice, Opie to this day associates door usage with food.

The other problem is timing. If you own a dog, you might be familiar with this script: "Opie, do you want to come in?" Opie does not want to come in. "Opie, are you sure?" Opie is sure. So we go into the living room, settle into our easy chairs and—scratch-scratch-scratch.

Hannah's issue is that she wants to, as Beth says, "Be with her people." If you have watched a dog show, you know that a bulldog is not in the hunting class, herding class or working class, they are simply listed as "companion dogs." This means they have no discernible, professional contribution to society. In the human world, they would be known as "consultants."

So "being with her people" is all fine and dandy, unless one people is inside and the other people is outside. Hannah is the only dog I know who can scratch to go out at the same time she's scratching to come in. This results in her standing astride the threshold, confused on matters of egress and ingress.

The flies and stink bugs are not confused, however, and 14 metric tons of them generally come rushing in while she's standing there making up her mind.

But at least the dogs have their reasons; the cat does not, other than the fact that watching us bounce up to get the door is good sport. Like the old cat Tom Quartz in Mark Twain's mining town, Juliet "never kitched a rat in her life— peared to be above it."

But this does not stop her from engaging in fantasy safaris, which apparently make her quite thirsty. She will squawk to come in, take exactly one lap of water and then squawk to go back out and resume the hunt.

Finally, it all came to a head. I sat the three animals down and explained the situation to them. From now on, they each would be allotted three coupons a day, each coupon being good for one exit and one enter.

Opie used up his first three coupons in about 10 minutes. He then tried to trade two of his next-week coupons for one of Hannah's today coupons. Hannah asked for a clarification. Did it count if her head and shoulders were out on the porch while the balance of the dog remained inside?

I'm pretty sure both are considering taking the matter to court—if someone will let them out.

A horse is a horse, of course, of course
Unless you need a mare to look like a stallion, of course
September 30, 2009

I got a casting call in the mail the other day—not for me, I don't have enough feet. But if they pay cash, I think I can help them out.

The notice went as follows:

"In preparation for the shooting later this year of the upcoming Walt Disney Pictures' movie 'Secretariat,' Mayhem Pictures, the producers of the film, will conduct an open, online 'casting call' for horses to portray the legendary 1973 Triple Crown winner."

"Mayhem Pictures?" Never mind, the point is that I happen to have a couple of subjects that I believe would be marvelous stars, and considering that they are currently eating me out of house and home, I would be more than happy to do my part, so to speak. Have saddle, will travel.

My first thought turned to my own mount Cappuccino, who has a movie star personality if ever there was. Gregarious, fun-loving, slightly air-headed—if served hay in her dressing room, she would want the green stalks removed.

But then Cappy is a full-figured girl, half thoroughbred, half draft horse. She can run like the wind, but when she does her mind tends to wander and she'll start looking all around, which is never a good thing considering her considerable size and limited braking action. Seeing her run gives you that uneasy feeling that you get when you see a tractor-trailer driver who's text messaging.

She's a sweetie, but because of her size, visitors are often terrified to be in the same barn with her—although as Beth says, if they had any sense they'd be more scared of the miniature horse Doodlebug, who is sort of the Chuckie of the equine world.

Many mornings, I walk out the door to see Beth's silhouette stalking high on a far-away ridge, a sure sign that the Little Puke, as I call him, has slipped his halter and made a successful getaway.

We have a mean old goose whose name I forget, and Doodlebug is the only creature in the farm who doesn't defer to the unpleasant bird. Should the goose give chase, the Little Puke will turn and twist its beak around to True North.

But the Secretariat casting call says that "a calm temperament is particularly key, especially when multiple takes are involved." Scratch Doodlebug. The only multiple thing he's capable of is fits.

So that leaves Beth's horse, Splendid Brooke, who has the disadvantage of being a mare instead of a colt and a bay instead of a chestnut. According to the casting call, "applicants need not feel that they must have an identical looking horse to be considered. We can do wonders with equine makeup for the white facial markings and the three white socks."

Maybe. If they can powder a bay into a chestnut well and good, but if they have something that can make a mare look like a stallion I don't want to know about it.

They do say they will need "at least two main Secretariats" and "perhaps four stand-ins." Who knew there was such a thing as a stunt horse? But if they need six total, that does increase our odds.

Heck, maybe all three of ours could be of use. Brooke as the main, in-his-prime Secretariat; Cappy as the disillusioned, washed-up Secretariat who has let himself go by gorging on banana, bacon and peanut butter sandwiches; and then the Little Puke as the old, cantankerous Secretariat who spends his time watching C-Span and cussing out the younger generation.

Hollywood could hardly ask for more.

Rooster that eats stink bugs not for sale at any price
October 6, 2009

I have a rooster for sale. The asking price is $1,000, firm.

All right, so as roosters go he isn't much to look at. No proud, imperial, feathered headdress of a rooster, he.

He's small, with bandy legs and no comb to speak of. An Araucana (were he a hen, he'd be the type that lays blue eggs), he's all white with no tail and his attempts at crowing sound like a tractor-trailer with malfunctioning air brakes. I call him Stink.

The name should be a clue to his elevated value, since he is a chicken whose preferred source of nutrition is stink bugs. He spends his days stalking the foundations of the smokehouse and summer kitchen, his head cocked at an angle that points his eyeball about 40 degrees above the horizon.

When he spots one of these prehistoric-looking insects, he performs, all in one graceful motion, a hop and a peck. The stink bug never stands a chance. He must consume 100 bugs or so a day, making me glad he's a rooster—I doubt anyone would eat any eggs from such a bird.

Those, like me, who were hoping the stink bug invasion of 2008 was a one-year anomaly have been sorely disappointed. Not only are they back, they seemed to have learned from last year's mistakes. This year, they seem much harder to kill.

A couple of weeks ago, I heard a shaky plea for help from Beth, who said we had a "big problem in the bathroom." I leapt into action, fearing an inundation of about 6 inches of water on the floor.

Imagine my relief when the problem only turned out to be several thousand stink bugs covering every bathroom surface.

Beth, curiously, did not share in my happiness.

She—otherwise the kindest, gentlest person on the planet—goes after the creatures with a vengeance. At first, she carried a gasoline-filled jar with her everywhere. When she would hold the jar underneath a bug, the fumes would make it dizzy and it would fall in, at which point Beth slammed the lid shut with a force generally associated with colliding asteroids.

In stink bug season, my nerves are always hanging on by a thread, because even nondescript conversations are punctuated by the violent concussions of a stink bug meeting its maker.

"I could take some hamburger out SLAM of the freezer tonight if you want SLAM Chili, or we could SLAM have that leftover tuna SLAM steak..."

She brought a somewhat startling droid behavior to the project: "Must kill stink bugs. Must kill stink bugs." Even the dogs seemed a bit unnerved to see mommy flying down the hall with a jug of gasoline and all the compassion of a medical waste incinerator.

Perhaps it does not need to be mentioned, but the smell of sting bugs rotting in gasoline is not pleasant. After objections from myself and her colleague Cindy, Beth switched to rubbing alcohol. So from an environmental standpoint, I congratulate her for going green when it comes to stinkbug eradication.

It was no small concession on her part. Last year, several readers suggested a spray of water and soap was effective against stink bugs, but Beth didn't buy in on the grounds that death by soap bubbles was "too good" for them.

When the jar is full, a pyre will be prepared in the fire pit and, with all the trappings of an ancient cult, we will have the Burning of the Stink Bugs and listen to their little corpses pop.

Beth seems surprised when I don't want to watch. So, even though my sense of smell isn't that good and they don't bother me too much, we both want the bugs gone, even if for different reasons.

As such, I've decided that Stink isn't for sale at any price.

Escaped convicts—no trouble here, doggone it

November 2, 2009

The linemen from Allegheny Energy were true professionals.

The dogs were not.

Some background:

We felt rather superior when we received the notice that you can sign up for an escaped-prisoner alert from the Division of Correction.

Little old ladies might need that, I thought, but not moi. First, I have a shotgun, although I cannot necessarily endorse its effectiveness.

The pellets make it out of the barrel in sharp order, but at 10 feet, they are growing short of breath. By 20 feet, they are panting. And at 30 feet, they are flat-out exhausted and looking to lie down for a rest.

Plus, I can never remember where I left the weapon. I'm hesitant to put it under the bed because I'm afraid I'd blow my own foot off some morning and I really hate dealing with open wounds before I've had my coffee.

So I just leave it around, and it could cause an awkward moment if I had to politely ask an escaped felon if he could hold on for a sec while I ransacked the house for my gun.

But no matter, because we have dogs.

They'd never hurt anyone, but they can bark a good game and Opie is about the size, shape and color of a bear, so he can be intimidating to the uninitiated.

Hannah the bulldog is territorial, but, strangely enough, only in matters of airspace. Buzzards, medevacs and one wayward parasailor have all been subjects of her wrath. The Goodyear blimp will never be able to swoop in and steal our—I'm trying to think of something we have worth stealing—our five-gallon buckets of walnuts while Hannah is on the job.

All right, so anyway, Beth wakes me up at 5 a.m. last week and says, "Something's going on in our lower pasture."

Sure enough, I look out the window and see what appear to be a dozen alien spaceship landing lights blazing away smack in the middle of the field.

Beth, knowing the way my mind works, looked at me and asked the only salient question she could at that point in time: "Do you think you can get a column out of this?"

No lie.

A quick investigation revealed the halogen lights belonged to a big truck and a backhoe that was digging up a large trench in the field. An Allegheny worker quickly explained: "Your neighbor lost power and the primary runs underground off of this pole."

I was still asleep enough that this explanation sounded perfectly fine to me.

On my way back up the hill, I ran into Beth, who asked what was up.

"Oh, the primary runs through the field," I said.

She was still asleep enough to say, "Oh, OK."

The linemen tidied everything up perfectly, and it was only later that we learned the poor fellows had been out there all night. Our neighbor's power blew during the late innings of the World Series, and apparently the crew had been up and down our driveway all through the early morning hours with heavy and noisy equipment, bucket trucks and spotlights, hunting for the problem.

It does not bother me that they did this. It does not bother me that we did not wake up while they did this. It bothers me that the dogs did not wake up.

Opie will go nuts at the kind, elderly gentleman who walks along the road collecting aluminum cans. Hannah about bursts at an aircraft at 30,000 feet. But when heaven and earth literally move beneath their eight collective feet?

We might as well put a sign out front, "Escaped felons welcome here."

Chuckles the rooster avoids date with death
Smartest chicken on Little Farm by the Creek impersonates hen to escape freezer
November 11, 2009

When I was a kid, the chickens we raised for meat were not "slaughtered." They were "dressed." Or "processed." The difference might have been lost on a chicken, but it made us feel better.

Why say that you are going to scald, pluck, gut, eviscerate or disembowel a chicken when you can simply say that you are going to "put it in the freezer?"

The terminology comes into play because we bought a run of 15 araucana chickens last summer, figuring on about half hens, half roosters. Instead, we got 11 boys and four girls.

There is no appreciation for males on a farm. Females are desired, coddled, swooned over and treasured. But if you're a boy, it's an inside view of an upright Amana for you.

The roosters' date with destiny was scheduled for Nov. 4, and for three days prior, I couldn't look any of them in the eye. We decided to keep one rooster for picturesque "crowing on a fencepost at dawn" purposes, but the rest had to go. (Stink, the stinkbug-eating chicken, was obviously the lucky boy.)

As all roosters do, the fellows would run around the place while shrieking, fighting, mauling hens and being truly sociable. The hens—including one I'd named Chuckles, for her clown-like, feathered sideburns—would sit in the coop all day to keep away from the crowing motorcycle gang on the outside.

So after the roosters had been duly dispatched, the hens cautiously began to emerge into the sunlight. They were understandably timid at first—all except Chuckles, who suddenly became as bold and fearless as Captain Cook.

The chicken followed me around like a dog, pecked at my feet, chased the other girls with spirit and then stretched her neck to its fullest—and crowed.

"You devious little fraud!" I thundered.

This is the absolute truth: For five months, the jerk had lived with the hens and acted like the hens. (S)he never joined in with the band of brothers outside, never crowed, never tried to mate with the other girls—never did anything to indicate she was a he.

But the day after we returned from the abattoir and he determined the coast was clear, oh brother, did he begin to make up for lost time.

Lacking practice, Chuckles' crows were a little rocky at first. But his ego exploded through the roof and he chased down every last hen, as if he were a cross between Foghorn Leghorn and Bill Clinton.

So now what? Two roosters almost always wind up with irreconcilable differences, so it would make sense to eliminate one. Stink's value and virtue are beyond reproach. Then we have Chuckles, whose resume includes deceit, duplicity, betrayal, dishonesty, subterfuge and a blackness of soul unparalleled among fowl. But, in him, we may also hold title to the wisest chicken to ever walk the earth.

Plus, there's an unwritten rule at Little Farm by the Creek that once you receive a name, you are safe from the butcher's knives. And he has those curious and wondrous locks that jut from his cheeks like Martin Van Buren experiencing an electrical shock.

So for now, let's just say that Chuckles is on double secret probation. We have another load of broiler chickens that have a date with the freezer in another week. Chuckles can shape up or get dressed. The choice is up to him.

Social events at our house go to the dogs
November 30, 2009

When normal people have guests, there are a standard number of questions to be answered. What do we serve? Which wine would be appropriate? Is the tablecloth clean? Where should people park? Do we force people to watch our stinkin' slide show of our trip to Dollywood before or after dessert?

We can't be bothered with these trivial matters because one question relegates all others to afterthoughts, and that question is: "What do we do with the dogs?"

Basically, this is an issue of limiting human-canine interface to the degree that the laws of physics will allow.

Perhaps it's because we have visitors infrequently. Perhaps it's because we have excessively exuberant dogs. Perhaps it was poor training on our part. Perhaps it's because people are always hesitant about dogs they do not know.

Whatever the case, whenever Hannah (bulldog) and Opie (bouvier) sense new meat on the premises, the encounter almost never goes well.

We always issue the standard caveat to any new visitor: "The dogs are friendly, but ..."

The devil is in the "but."

I remember an old Marmaduke cartoon, where the postman is breaking in a rookie. Walking up the drive, he points to the animal and says, "That's Marmaduke. He doesn't bite, but oohhh brother."

In a sentence, that's Opie. Oh brother, where arf thou? At about eye level, generally, given that he's half dog, half pogo stick.

If we don't catch them in time, they're both out the door like artillery—usually to the sound of car doors being slammed shut, as visitors consider whether our company is worth the trouble. Through some miracle of science, the word "no" has been purged from their vocabularies. We say "no jump," and they hear "jump." We say "no lick" and they hear "lick."

Even for self-described "dog people," Opie, at more than 100 pounds, can cause real problems, especially when he hits his target at 40 feet a second.

We barely have time to get out a frantic, "Opie, don't ..." before the sound of air being forced from lungs reaches our ears, followed a split second later by the sound of someone being pinned, with force, against his car. Many people have left our house with a human-shape imprint stamped into their sheet metal. If we hear a "thump," we don't worry so much. But when we hear "thump-thump" we know it's time to call the body shop.

And while Opie is working the shoulders, Hannah is taking out the knees. It's a pretty effective team, if one can appreciate it at a distance.

We have two buildings, home and office, suitable for canine incarceration, but that presents a separate risk. A forced detainment only serves to wind their springs tighter and tighter, and if by some chance we need to go inside, they'll shoot out with exponential violence, leaving the screen door impotently swaying back and forth on one hinge.

Some people are braver than others. Or less worldwise. They'll say, "Oh, don't make the doggies stay inside, we'll be fine."

Beth and I usually exchange a level glance at this point, and say, "No, you don't want that." If they insist, there's nothing much we can do except shrug and open the door to the four-footed projectiles.

We have noticed that, unlike the dogs, the people in question generally catch on to the true meaning of "no" the first time and do not make the same request twice.

Chuckles' temperament is no laughing matter
January 5, 2010

Most businesses have a policy of listening to the public, of maintaining strict adherence to the ideal that the customer is always right, and of being receptive to any and all comments from the clientele.

In fact, early on, I decided that my response to any public input would be to cover my ears and chant "La-la-la."

Unfortunately for me, I deviated from this policy when an overwhelming number of people called and wrote, telling me to spare our young Aracauna rooster named Chuckles from the chopping block. In wavy dream sequence, let me remind you that Chuckles pretended to be a (valuable, egg-laying) hen up until the day that we sent all the other roosters but one (Stink) to be processed for future sautés.

Chuckles is all white, with no tail worth mentioning and two mutton chop-like tufts of feathers protruding perpendicular from his cranial region. "Cranial" might be a stretch, since that suggests the presence of a brain looming somewhere aft of the eyeballs. He can't even crow worth a lick.

Chuckles is possessed of a temperament so vile, so absurd, that my first instinct was to wring the little jerk's neck at first opportunity. In fact, Beth recently had to leave town on business and I was resolved to dispatch Chuckles in her absence. But I didn't, partly because of a thumbs-up from you Roman hoards and partly because bad animals have a habit of making for good writing subjects.

In this sense, Chuckles has not disappointed.

On her return, Beth—who, frankly makes PETA look like a bunch of bloodthirsty Visigoths—seemed mildly disappointed that the rooster was still stalking the grounds of Little Farm by the Creek.

And stalk he did. And does. Speaking honestly, there is nothing about Chuckles that can be loved, aside from his picturesque appearance. Part bully, part coward, part airhead, part instigator, part—well, picture Glenn Beck with feathers. My enduring memory of the bird is of him running at full speed from atrocity he himself has created.

He never apologizes, he never repents, he never owns up to his failings; he just runs. He runs from the big hens who rebuff his attempts at romance. He runs from Stink, the virtuous eater of stink bugs and enforcer of justice. No wonder about that, since Stink routinely beats the snot out of Chuckles whenever he gets out of line—which is to say about eight times daily.

Chuckles picks on the young hens who are smaller than he—makes their lives miserable, in fact. A recurring vignette is a bloodcurdling shriek pulsating through one of the barns. Then comes a secondary shriek. I'll get to the window in time to see Chuckles heading for the hills at high speed. In a couple of seconds, Stink will strut out of the barn with a look that says "... and stay out!"

He doesn't, of course, He slinks back to his position of tormentor in chief the second Stink turns his back.

I try to feel sorry for the poor bird, but I can't even do that. I know there are other creatures in this world that must go through life as Chuckles does—despised, unappreciated, insecure and abused. So sometimes, when no one is looking, I'll slip him a little extra corn and say, "Here you go Chuckles—there have been times when I've been in that situation myself."

All the variations of animal farm in winter
February 10, 2010

If this is climate change, you can count me out. I'm so terrorized that I'm tempted to go out and cut off the engine to my SUV, which has been idling in the driveway for the last eight days, just so hints of auto-body paint will show through, reminding me where it's parked.

Who knew that plastic grocery bags could lead to this?

We had to change the name of our farm from Little Farm by the Creek to Little Farm by the Glacier.

And since it's a little farm, I don't have any of that manly snow-removing equipment. All I've got is a shovel and an ax. The shovel is for cutting paths and the ax is for burying in the skull of any animal that is of the opinion that I'm not bringing the hay in fast enough. Or for chipping 6 inches of ice out of the watering troughs, although the former, at times, might certainly seem more satisfying.

Fortunately, we have a network of real farmers who help us out. Unlike corporate America, these country folk can be depended on and even show up unasked.

But even the alpacas, who believe that life at 14,000 feet up in the Andes is just a good swimming climate, have been staying in their shed.

Hannah, the bulldog, hates it the most. She hates the feel of ice on her dainty little feet and we have to get her out of the house to do her business with a water cannon.

The donkeys are not happy, because they have to share a barn with the cows, who only come in when the weather gets extreme. They react to stress the same way as people—by eating. So carrying all this

82

water and hay has pretty much bulked up my arms to the point where I make John Basedow look like Woody Allen.

Even the chickens are subdued, and they are generally about as subduable as seagulls. We haven't seen the geese in weeks. We assume they're down on the creek somewhere, but they might have hooked up with a V of Canada cousins and headed south.

Juliet, the Siamese cat, hates the snow, but unlike the other animals, she blames us for its presence. Like we ordered this from L.L. Bean or something just to tick her off. Possibly, since we jump at her every whim, she is of the opinion that we could do something about it if we really wanted, and the fact that we don't means that she'd probably be better off in a cage at the animal shelter eating bags of donated Friskies.

The only critters who actually enjoy the stuff are the two young Toggenburg goats, Nicholas and Alvin, the mini horse named Doodlebug and—you have probably guessed by now—the bouvier de Flanders named Opie, whose only complaint is that we don't bring the good old-fashioned white stuff indoors so he can play in it there, too.

In this regard, however, he does a pretty good job on his own. Despite our best toweling efforts, his woolly fur generally carries in it enough snow to blanket an Olympic-style giant slalom ski course.

If we're sitting around the house (not that there's been much time for that) and see an organically expanding pool of water on the living room floor, we assume there must be a dog in there somewhere and fish him out before attacking the snowmelt with a wet vac.

At which point, the animal will happily bound back outside where it's 2 degrees and return later in an icicle costume so other-worldly and eclectic that Lady Gaga only wishes she'd dreamed up.

Just one more reason to own dogs, if you're on the fence.

Bulldog takes on conehead personality

February 22, 2010

I'd seen those embarrassing lampshade collars that dogs sometimes have to wear to prevent them from chewing on an injured leg, and always thought to myself indignantly, "No animal of mine will ever ..."

Yeah, well.

Hannah, the blonde bulldog, chews on her paws when they're healthy, so when a small growth needed to be removed from one of her aft appendages, there was really no reason to think she would leave the stitched-up wound alone.

We gave her every chance, but after she chewed through enough bandages to upholster four or five Egyptian kings, we knew there was no choice.

Affixing the collar wasn't easy, since bulldogs do not have anything resembling a neck. It was kind of like trying to lasso an egg.

Needless to say, she looked ridiculous and she knew it. When we took her outside, she hung her head as she walked, which was poor judgment, since the lampshade began gathering snow like a plow until her head became packed with frozen material.

The first of our other animals to see her was the cat. Hannah was sitting mournfully in the kitchen when Juliet came scampering in from an unsuccessful hunt under the bird feeder.

One glance at the accessorized bulldog and the Siamese slammed on the brakes, threw her back skyward and looked for all the world like one of those Halloween kitties whose fur indicates an encounter with an electrical socket. After one, long obligatory hiss, Juliet proceeded to exit the kitchen with a quickness.

Meanwhile, Hannah, the world's most passive-aggressive dog, was learning to play the collar like a flute. She filled the house with pitiful sighs, she purposefully knocked into breakables with her collar, and her large sad eyes appeared to be dripping down her face.

Now, if you know me at all, you understand that I would not be writing about Hannah's condition unless it affected me.

So pitiful was the animal that Beth decided she needed to set up a bed on the floor of the living room so she could sleep while comforting the dog.

I just shrugged and plodded up the stairs to bed that night, and there, sitting on the bed waiting for me was—the cat.

She had a list of grievances long as your arm, and no one was going to get any sleep until every last one had been addressed.

Topping the list was the fact that Juliet likes to sleep on Beth's back (yes, I know, I know; just leave it, OK?), and tonight the cat's own personal hot water bottle was missing. I was not about to play futon to a furball, so I rolled over on my side, my back to the rasping creature.

I could feel her paw tapping on my head. When that didn't work, she adjusted her starboard whisker set to ever-so-gently tickle my neck. Next came the ear-licking. Then she walked back and forth over top of me a few times, until I scooted to the very edge of the bed.

She stopped her overt torture for a while, but I could feel her sitting there, staring at me. Then, kathunk, she jumped off the bed.

This was worse in some ways, because I couldn't tell where she was or what she had planned next.

Her plans materialized soon enough as a full, claws at the ready, frontal assault that failed, barely, to pull me off the bed, but was more effective in landing all the covers in a heap on the floor.

It went on that way until well after midnight. Down below, I could hear the bulldog snoring happily away. So I don't care how they look —next time I'm wearing the collar and the dog can deal with the cat.

Calf acting uncowlike does have personality
March 1, 2010

I've become quite wary of animals with "personality." Personality makes it sound like a good thing, but this is never the case.

Bette Midler has personality. Jon Stewart has personality. In animals, "personality" is used to cover up serious character defects.

Just because a dog chews your leather-bound Shakespeare classics to shreds and then throws them up all over the cat doesn't mean he has personality. It just means he's a bad dog.

So give me an animal with no personality any day.

This is why I assumed cows and I would be a good fit. Cows don't chew up your slippers, scratch your furniture, kick down stall doors, chase cars or do much of anything.

You walk up to a cow in the field and she'll stare at you—and look as if she is perfectly willing to stare at you for the next six or seven years if need be—until you walk away.

Only one member of our small herd has ever escaped, and that only happened when he fell asleep leaning up against the fence and it eventually gave way under his weight.

So when the phone rang in the hotel room at 6 a.m. last week (with a frazzled Beth on the other end of the line), I knew it had to be some critter-related issue. But I also assumed it wouldn't be about the cows.

"It's about the cows," she said.

"I knew it. You tell Opie that the moment I get home, he's in big trouble and he's going to have to deal with, it's about the WHAT?"

"Cows."

"What can they possibly be doing at this hour of the morning?"

"Well, have a calf, for one thing."

I searched the memory banks. Sometime last spring I did seem to recall that we'd taken a stab at breeding our two Belted Galloway heifers named Cleopatra and Heifertiti. But the young, inexperienced bull, whom we called Dan, was always finding himself on the wrong side of the creek, getting into the wrong end of the feeder and mounting the wrong end of the cows. He was just one "Oh, a wise guy; nyuk nyuk" away from completing the full effect.

He was quite handsome, but like a lot of pretty boys didn't always have the mental firepower to match. In fact, Beth swears that Cleopatra took one look at Dan and resolved on the spot that this hapless youngster would never father her children.

Well, at some point he must have gotten her drunk, or something. Because sure enough, when I arrived home some hours later, there was a Very Small Cow in standard Belted Galloway dress (picture a cow with the markings of an Oreo cookie) hopping all about, pestering her uncles, chasing the chickens and being truly sociable.

It might seem surprising, but behavior-wise, there is no appreciable difference between a calf and a puppy.

In keeping with our Egyptian sobriquet motif, we wanted to name her Princess something or other, but so goofy was her behavior that nothing cooked up in the Valley of the Kings seemed to fit.

Frankly, when she wasn't nursing or sound asleep, she was full of beans. Which is why we gave her the name of Princess Beans, something I'm sure I'll come to regret at multiple points in her future life. As we speak, she's doing sprints around the round-bale holder and engaging in other un-cowlike behavior.

All I can do is hope that Princess Beans grows up fast.

Birth of farm animals 'deer' to my heart
March 22, 2010

People say the miracle of birth is a beautiful thing. I do not say this. I think the miracle of birth is a whole lot of ick, especially as it pertains to farm animals.

In truth, I'm not a big fan of miracles of any kind. The parting of the Red Sea sounded like an invitation to get stuck in the mud—and can you imagine being a biblical insurance adjuster hearing about the Walls of Jericho?

"Let me get this straight, they circled the city seven times, blew their horns and then WHAT happened?"

So as previously noted, I was out of town for the arrival of Princess Beans, the Belted Galloway calf that is now a month old, daughter to Cleopatra.

Next up was Heifertiti, who delivered another little girl named Princess Tina, in honor of our neighbor who helped out with Princess Beans when I was away.

I am starting to appreciate cattle more, especially in the way that they deliver their young. Where the goats bellow and crave attention, cows are the absentee landlords of the birthing process.

Heifertiti, bless her, got as far away from our house as the farm would allow. Unfortunately, she was pretty close to our neighbor Becky's house when she called up miracle central. Imagine opening up your curtain Saturday morning before you've had your coffee and seeing—oh, never mind.

That morning, I'd noticed that Heifertiti was missing, so I went searching for her. By the time of my arrival, the more meaningful arrival had already taken place.

I sensed mild disappointment in Beth, who likes to assemble "birthing kits" that have an estimated 4,379 surgical and sanitary items at the ready, and to organize the blessed event right down to the disposal of the yuk.

The cow managed it all on her own, and even rigorous hunting on Beth's part revealed no afterbirth. She is curious about these things. I am not.

"I wonder what happened to it? Oh, I wonder if she ate ..."

"HUSH UP."

So the calves are doing fine at this point and learning about the world around them.

Up until now, Princess Beans and Princess Tina had been pretty sure all animals were like them. Hang around. Get fed. Graze. Hang around some more. Top speed, 5 mph.

And that's when they first saw the deer: Eight of them in all, running full speed across the ridge. The cattle were lined up on the far end of the hill perpendicular to where the deer were approaching. In the middle of the line were the calves.

Deer must not look too far ahead because they didn't see the bovine barrier until the 50-foot mark—at which point they slammed on the brakes with some authority, deer piling into the backs of other deer like cars on a foggy interstate.

Quite a standoff ensued, both forces staring at each other and planning action (action might be too strong a word in the case of the cows —the simple act of turning their heads can take a week).

Finally, the deer made a headlong charge at the middle of the line. Poor Princess Beans, for one, was pretty sure she was a goner. She flopped on the ground, sprung up and pinwheeled her spindly legs cartoon-style, which provided little in the way of locomotion.

The deer, of course, were bigger chickens than the cows. It was all a feint, and at the last second, they dodged right and jumped the fence. Apparently they have better things to do than watch live births, as well.

Animals are only human after all
April 5, 2010

I started collecting critters under the working theory that they were, in some ways, superior to humans.

While acknowledging that they might not have our mental horse-power, I also assumed they lacked petty, human traits such as jealousy, vindictiveness, selfishness and the like.

Unfortunately, this is not the case. If anything, animals can trump most of our undesirable characteristics, and the only reason we don't hear more about it is that animals do not stupidly hire press agents and media consultants to compound the problem.

The alpacas spend all day spitting at each other; goats will chase other goats away from the haymow, even though there's plenty to go around; donkeys will scream if we dare feed another animal before they have had theirs; and a chicken of ours named Hattie will come up and peck at the back of your leg if you are favoring another animal with too much attention.

But these are minor vices compared to the geese—two of the most lawless and unlovable birds that ever roamed the face of the earth.

They are as loud as a band of drunken pirates and mean as sin. Ralphie will lower his head and charge any animal, up to and including the draft horse.

They used to hang out by an old smokehouse that we converted into a tack room. It's filled with saddles, bridles, leather straps, crops, riding boots and chains—stuff that would only excite a horse person, or a member of the Republican National Committee.

But it was also filled with stinkbugs, which might have been an appealing quality for the geese. During the snows of the Great Winter of 2010, however, the geese broke camp and went to live down on the creek—a watercourse being more maneuverable to a goose than 2 feet of snow.

There, they made life miserable for any other creature that might try to move in, including ducks, Canada geese and blue herons.

Then, one day, another family of domestic geese showed up, for reasons that have yet to be established. Compared to our pair of barroom brawlers, this was a family of Sunday school geese.

They are gorgeous birds and perfectly coifed (ours tend to be rather plain with red, satanic eyeballs and feathers akimbo). The new family has good manners. They come and go, never wearing out their welcome. Our geese scream for bread and hiss ungratefully when they get it. The newcomers ask politely for a treat and honk with thanksgiving on its appearance. The old geese are always stirring for a fight; the new geese live in harmony with all comers.

However, these new geese do not tolerate bullies. Ralphie pushed his luck with the new head goose once too often, and instead of backing away, the new guy took up the fight. And what a fight—wings spread, feathers flying and a volume that exceeded that of low-flying aircraft. When all was said and done, Ralphie was running for his life down the hill to the creek.

I never thought I would live to see the day when he was whipped, but here it was.

Then, the other day, I came home and there were Ralphie and Edwina, sitting way upstream in seclusion, cigarettes hanging out the corners of their mouths, and a look of depression, puzzlement and weak defiance on their faces.

Closer to the house were the usurpers, the perfect family, saying grace over a picnic lunch and doing charity work for the poor. Like Mary Poppins, they were perfect in almost every way.

But something made me want to go back and give our geese a hug. Sure, they're thugs and outlaws, and cuddly as snakes—but they are our thugs. Family, as such.

In the end, maybe we're just too much alike.

The goop and the poop about goats
April 26, 2010

When I got into this whole gentleman farmer detail, it was with the clear understanding that life would go like this:

I'd sit there with a mint julep and a fine plug of chewing tobacco in my khaki trousers (to be clear, I would be in my trousers, not the chewing tobacco) and Polo button-down, and I would be saying things such as "You there, whatever your name is, do please feed the donkeys" or "I say, old chap, the rose bush that I am beholding has a rather long thistle that I so wish though shouldst trim."

Unfortunately, the truth is that my drinks have been reduced to turnip juice, the only thing I chew is a gum that hasn't been popular since the 1920s and my wardrobe is the Schmidt line from Tractor Supply. They sell jeans for $12 a pair, and they are worth it.

I always assumed there was money in farming. That's always the way. You reckon there's money in everything, except what you are doing at the moment.

But really, it seemed logical that the animals did all the work. A well-bred Toggenburg dairy goat, for example, would bring in $200. All I'd have to do was sit back and watch the pregnancy advance and the money pile up in my pocket.

Even better, goats have twins, which would multiply my wealth exponentially.

This logic was fine as far as it went.

Sadly, as my logic always is, it was flawed. I sort of assumed that goats—like the welfare mothers in Ronald Reagan's anecdotes—popped out a kid once every three days.

So I calculated my profits. I gave much away, on paper, to charity. I built a pool. I put up a new barn, installed automatic waterers and laid in a three-month supply of mint juleps.

But reality presented its problems. Being your typical male, I assumed a pregnancy was a snapshot, when in truth it is an oil painting. I never believed that a goat could sit around being pregnant for so long while producing squadoosh.

All the while, we were feeding our four mama goats an estimated $3,573 worth of hay and another $7,249 worth of grain.

But finally, the big day had come. I heard this noise coming from the pasture, and I said to my goat what I assume—never having had any children of my own—every husband says to his near-birth-giving wife: "Would you shut up? I'm trying to watch the game."

When I finally realized what was happening, I rushed into the field to help and was rewarded with two armloads of glop encased in what looked to me to be the shrink-wrap that you see at your supermarket meat counter.

"Oh, this could be handy," I thought, before the plastic broke and out jumped two living, breathing creatures that looked hopefully up at me, as if I could help them with their problems.

I pointed to their mom.

"Ask her," I said.

All the while, my arms dripping with goo, I was thinking about how the final selling price of these little goats would not equal what it cost us to feed their mamas for a month.

But somehow, as the wet little tykes looked up to me for guidance and uttered the first happy bleats of their little lives, the money involved was the last thing on my mind.

This kid really milks his mom for all she's worth

May 17, 2010

This spring, we were ... I'm reaching here, but I think the word is "blessed" ... with six baby goats, none of which are lacking in energy, enthusiasm or conviction in his or her beliefs.

Their beliefs are limited to three items, those being eat, sleep and create a general terror that can likely be heard for miles around.

They take breakfast at 6 a.m., and for the next two hours, the barn and pasture are filled with a variety of crashes, bangs and bleats in a cacophony that would make a human day-care center sound like a yoga class.

Naturally, I would wake up in the middle of the night with the singular thought: Must. Sell. Goats.

The worst (not necessarily for us, but for his mother) was a young buckling that was always, and I mean always, hungry. He would nurse until his mother, Hillary, would say "enough," but did this discourage him? Oh, no. He would chase Hillary around the pasture for hours, looking to latch on to her udder, buzzing the doe from all angles and allowing her no peace.

So annoyingly persistent was his pursuit that I wound up naming him Horsefly.

Hillary, named after the climber, is a pretty good athlete in her own right, but she was no match for little Horsefly, who could have given the Kenyans a run for their marathons.

She got a brief rest when I milked her in the evenings. She'd never been a big fan of milking before, but having her child locked out of the room gave her some peace that she seemed to cherish.

Afterward, I would open the door and, sure enough, there was Horsefly, happily wagging his tail with a frenzy and greeting his mom with, "I'm glad to see you're BACK; I've been waiting to SEE you again." And Hillary would freeze in the doorway and go mildly catatonic.

So you can imagine my relief and hers when a wonderful couple answered our advertisement about young goats for sale.

Of course, things for me are never this easy.

I was behind on chores and was racing around to be finished throwing hay by the time of Paula and Frank's arrival. I was just about done when I couldn't help but notice a 4-foot snake that was sunning himself in the paddock.

I am not permitted to kill these vipers, per instructions from the management, so I hastily grabbed him by the neck and headed for the driveway—just as our guests were pulling into the parking lot.

It is a testament to their tolerance that they did not immediately do a 180 and go fishtailing back down the lane, spraying gravel in their wake.

Here I was, wearing threadbare farm clothes, hadn't shaved in about four days, with a pitchfork in one hand and a writhing snake in the other. I froze. I knew this had to be an unspeakably picturesque introduction to Little Farm by the Creek, and feared I might have cost us a sale.

Fortunately, Paula and Frank were quite understanding, and Beth was there to clean up the mess. As I relocated Mr. Snake, she took them to the barn, where they were greeted by two blurs flashing in front of the barn doo —Hillary, and then Horsefly hot on her tail.

In the end, they decided to take Horsefly and his sister, and these are two very lucky goats. (And it needs to be noted that Hillary, not exactly being Mother of the Year material, did not miss them a bit.)

As we were sitting around talking that afternoon, Beth had only one request for the goat's upbringing: "Can you please name him something other than Horsefly?"

To that point, I had no idea that my creative efforts were so unappreciated.

Talking turkey
May 31, 2010

When a friend told Mark Twain that he was going to a Yiddish theater to dine with a party that included a minister, a Catholic bishop, an Indian Buddhist and a Confucian Chinese scholar, the great writer replied, "Well, there's only one thing you need to make the party complete—either Satan or me."

This is sort of why we got some turkeys.

We already had noisy chickens, obnoxious geese and a wild mallard that seems to be willing to trade in the uncertainties of nature for a seat at the domestic corn trough.

With turkeys, there are two ways you can go. Commercial hybrid varieties grow rapidly and provide an abundance of white meat. Heritage breeds, on the other hand, are said to have a richer flavor and they are better at foraging off the land, meaning they are cheaper to feed.

The commercial breeds aren't as self-sufficient and, as I understand it, have nothing in the way of survival skills. They tend to sit around and swell up to massive proportions, sort of like an above-ground rutabaga.

This is where Beth and I part company. I view the above statement as a positive, while she likes critters with a little more character. To me, character is another word for trampling all over the farm and getting into trouble. But, being a dark-meat fan, I was finally won over to a heritage breed known as Bourbon Reds.

Through the first few weeks of their lives, I didn't get much involved in their upbringing. Every few days, Beth would implore me to come out to the turkey barn "to see how fast they're growing," but other than that I was pretty much like the father in "Cats in the Cradle."

It couldn't last, and it didn't.

By the time they reached the size of elongated softballs, my dubious skills were called upon to build them an outdoor enclosure so they could get some sun, eat grass and bugs, and pitch horseshoes, or whatever it is turkeys do for amusement.

So we spent the better part of two days constructing what I believed to be a state-of-the-art turkey yard, complete with easy-access doors to the barn, catwalks to the pasture and an electric-net poultry fence.

On completion, we rousted them out of the barn and into the grass, which they seemed to thoroughly enjoy. Satisfied, we walked back to the house. But on hearing something out of the ordinary, we turned around to see the whole flock of long-necked little buzzards standing there in the yard and staring up at us quizzically in order to learn the next activity, as if we were social directors at a day-care center.

Turns out, turkey feathers make the birds impervious to electric shock, and even if this were not the case, the heritage breeds are good fliers and have no trouble gaining the necessary elevation to foil any fence.

Worse (for me anyway, Beth thinks it's cute) these speckled, strawberry blond little varmints are like dogs—they follow you everywhere you go. You can't shake them. And at this age they chirp with the consistency and melodiousness of a chronically squeaking wheel.

They find everything interesting, which would indicate intelligence, but this is not the case. Although superficially curious, you learn pretty quick that the switch is on, but the batteries are dead.

And they're kind of eerie. There's something very "Jurassic Park" about the raptors and they seem to share one brain among them "Jurassic Park" meets "Babes in Toyland" might be more accurate. So they robotically follow me, and all of us are followed by the cat, who Does Not Approve of this latest development.

Can't say that I do, either.

What's this I hear about a noise ordinance?
June 21, 2010

Here's what turning 50 means to me: Twelve days ago, I would have been strongly opposed to the proposed Washington County noise ordinance. Today, I am strongly in favor of it.

It's an age thing; if you're younger than 50, you wouldn't understand. The great paradox is that I can't hear much of anything anymore, but everything that I CAN hear is always too loud.

So the County Commissioners have been fielding complaints from residents over loud music coming from bars and a bed and breakfast, and they believe a noise ordinance might be in order.

Before addressing that, I have a serious issue that needs to be addressed: Where has this bed and breakfast been all my life? I always hated B&Bs because everything was always so ghostly quiet. You drop a doily on the floor and the sound causes everyone to stop and stare at you as if you'd just posed nude for Guideposts magazine, or something.

The City of Hagerstown already has a noise ordinance, but the county does not, which isn't uncommon. I remember a commissioner in another county long ago who—when a resident showed up to complain about noise—once remarked that in the county, "I can sit on my porch and beat my drum all night long and no one can do anything about it."

(The thought that, as a sitting commissioner, HE could have done something about it did not appear to have crossed his mind.)

Hagerstown's noise ordinance states: "It shall be unlawful for any person to make, continue or cause to be made or continued any unreasonably loud noise or any noise which either annoys, disturbs, injures or endangers the comfort, repose, health, peace or safety of others."

As someone who is always getting my repose jacked with, I can relate. We live in a quarry and a drag strip, for crying out loud (but not too loud, lest I be arrested). Of course, being a guy, I don't really consider the sound of powerful engines to be noise.

I am glad that the noise laws do seem to specify "any person," as opposed to "any animal"—in which case, we'd be toast. The sound of two chickens fighting over the same nest, for example, is something everyone ought to hear once, but not more often. It's like two big mommas fighting over the last two-for-one lavender Spandex sweat pants set at 6 a.m. on Black Friday.

And they are like the interior of a Cadillac next to the geese, who fight anything that moves and, lacking traditional weapons of brass or steel, use their vocal cords as a substitute.

Our ongoing pork project is also a decibel buster. The Gloucestershire Old Spots named Tillie and Chester do a lot of sleeping, which is a good thing because when they're awake, they fight like Ricky and Lucy. Or maybe they're playing; it's really kind of hard to tell with a pig. Whatever, it is shrill and it is loud and usually involves a dispute over the possession of some foodstuff.

But the noisiest of all are the donkeys. To characterize a donkey's call as a mere "heehaw" is like saying Rep. Joe Barton is "reality challenged." Their ear-splitting brays echo and rebound off the hills, gathering volume and momentum, drowning out the sound of dragsters and rock crushers alike. If the operators of these machines have in any way had their repose damaged, I offer my keen apologies.

Turkeys disprove theory of evolution
July 21, 2010

Afforded a little extra time from finishing chores early on Tuesday, I sat with a cup of coffee in what used to be a backyard, but now, thanks to the drought, resembles an abandoned shopping center parking lot. I don't mow anymore so much as I pluck.

I put my feet up on the patio table, watched the cattle munch at the round bale, saw the goats stretching out in the barn for a nap and listened to the gentle hum of the alpacas. Of course, this peaceful postcard of a setting didn't last. It never does anymore. I saw dust rising from the west and heard the watery chirps, trills and chortles that could only mean one thing: The turkeys had arrived.

I don't know whose bright idea it was to free range seven Bourbon Red turkeys—which are now about the size of buzzards and growing fast—but next time, I promise they will be imprisoned in a watertight container. Underground. In leg irons.

They are interesting enough birds to watch, but I swear I don't know how they stay alive. They have no skills of any kind. For no reason, they will take off, sprinting at full speed across the pasture, as if they've just been invited to spend the evening with Eva Mendes and a swimming pool full of Jello.

Then, all at once, all seven of them will stop dead in their tracks, reason unknown. They peer around trying to figure out who they were following and why. But it is a dead errand, for they're all followers, all following, even if they are only following their fellow followers. Or something like that.

I've known lots of dense people in my life who kind of made up for it by being spectacular athletes. But neither is this a turkey strength. The males like to puff out their feathers for the lady folk, which gives them that traditional Thanksgiving look.

One Tom decided he was going to show off to a hen this week while sitting on a paddock fence. But it was poor judgment. He looked deep in the hen's eyes, stuck out his breast and puffed up to full splendor— then lost his balance and fell off the fence. I picked him up and put him back on his perch. I knew how he felt. I've been in that situation myself.

Walking around the yard, a band of turkeys much resembles the old Monty Python "Twit of the Year" competition. Everything distracts them—water buckets, weeds, birdbaths. Next to them, a person with ADD looks like Boris Spassky.

So when I was sitting on the veranda with my feet up, it was only a matter of time until my propped-up lower extremities caught the eye of one of the hens. She studied my cargo shorts. She sized up my hamstrings. She gazed at my socks as intently as if she were considering getting a pair just like them at Costco.

Finally, knowing no better, I suppose, she decided that my shins would make as good a perch as any. So up she hopped, teetering back and forth on my legs and sinking her prehistoric talons in to the bone, causing no small degree of discomfort. Still, it wouldn't do to shake her off since this ordinarily flighty creature was putting so much faith in me.

She didn't seem terribly worried. She settled in, clucking, pecking my kneecaps until they bled, picking dead skin off her wing and being quite sociable.

Despite what has to be classified as a rather hideous face, a turkey does have eyes that are soft, inquisitive and almost doelike. You want to think there's a being in there somewhere that has thoughts, feelings and some degree of animal intelligence. But after she's stared at you for a couple of minutes, it becomes apparent that just beyond those eyes, it's solid concrete.

I let her stay as long as she wanted. If she's not scared of me by now, there is no hope for her.

Goats, pigs compete for overconditioned kudos
July 26, 2010

I learned a new word at the agricultural fair last week, which I believe will be a help to many of us in the greater Hagerstown area. The word is "overconditioned."

It came up during the dairy goat competition, when the judge felt that one of the animals had been laying in a bit heavily on the sweet feed. But he did not come out and say that the animal was a bit fat; instead, he said the goat was "overconditioned."

Brilliant.

I could stand to drop 10 or 15 pounds myself, but I am not obese. I am simply overconditioned. In fact, I am wearing a pair of my "overconditioned jeans" as we speak. If it gets much worse, I'll have to go to an overconditioning farm.

Do these pants make me look overconditioned?

We have one goat at the farm that is overconditioned beyond belief, but only because she's a jerk and chases everyone else away from the hay. We keep her in a pen with a couple of wethers that are of no more use than pets and an ancient goat with a Merlin-like beard who is little more than a pasture ornament.

I call this paddock the one with the "loser goats," a term Beth doesn't like.

The productive animals are kept elsewhere, and the daughter (Abbie) of one of the Toggenburgs—now owned by a couple of young friends who live nearby—was in the show.

Abbie placed third in her class, which sounds good until you consider that there were only three animals in the competition. It's like coming in second in a U.S. presidential race. After we got home, I had a talk with Heidi, her mom. I told her that her daughter had brought shame on the farm, but Heidi was too busy working on some overconditioning of her own to listen.

But I didn't sit down to write about goats. I wanted to write about pigs, specifically the Hot Dog Pig Races at the county fair, a presentation of F and F Productions out of Jackson, N.J.

Why, why, why, am I such a sucker for these things? Everything about it screamed "Run away at full speed," but I couldn't. Maybe it was the trailer with the giant inflatable pig on top. Maybe it was the guy selling plastic checkered racing flags and waving around a pink pig puppet to the sound of pig-themed music. Maybe it was the names they gave to the pigs—Jerry Swinefeld, Lindsay Loham, Kevin Bacon, etc.

According to the company's website (yes, I was that obsessed that I looked them up), "These awkward, but cute and cuddly racing animals fascinate spectators. Real crowd pleasers, these natural comedians bolt from the starting gate and race around the track snorting and squealing, stubby legs churning and curly tails sailing along behind."

Well, it was something like that, I guess.

In a way, I feel bad about critiquing the pig races, since by my very presence I skewed the average spectator age upward by about 20 years.

The audience consisted of:

1. A lot of kids, who absolutely loved it.

2. A lot of parents of kids, who had an excuse to be there and consequently were free to relax and enjoy.

3. A handful of childless adults trying their best not to look guilty.

Each race took about eight seconds as the pigs quickly galloped around a short loop. In between was just a lot of good, old-fashioned carnival barkering. Personally, I would have liked to see longer races —or maybe a porkathalon that would have forced them to swim or ride bikes.

With short little races like this, it is easy for a pig to get overconditioned.

This Thanksgiving promises to be the best ever
Seven Dweebs that populate farm are all named Dopey
August 25, 2010

I feel safe in saying that we will not be raising any more Bourbon Red heritage turkeys at Little Farm by the Creek. Beth and I have independently come to the conclusion that it's just one of those supposedly fun and cool agricultural pursuits that we will never do again.

The advantage of a Bourbon Red is that its flavor is reported to be richer than the standard, dry-breasted turkey bred to produce massive amounts of white meat, even in its eyeballs.

I no longer care. It doesn't matter if the Bourbon Reds taste like a caviar and truffle taco, no bird can have a flavor appealing enough to offset the headache of raising them.

There have been days when I could have cheerfully strangled any or all of the Seven Dweebs that populate the farm and follow me around like I am some kind of Pied Piper for poultry.

Forget everything you've heard about Ben Franklin wanting the turkey to be our national bird. All this proves is that the Founding Fathers were on acid.

It is not enough to say that they are ignorant, for it is an uncommonly pure ignorance, distilled from stupidity and decanted from idiocy. When they wake up in the morning, they will have forgotten overnight that their coop is well-supplied with food and water. I have to lead them out of the turkey barn then turn around about 50 feet later and lead them back in so that they will eat.

Invariably, they will look at the feeder as if seeing it for the first time, chortling in shock and happiness at the same bounty that they have had every morning—but apparently have maintained no mental tracking code of—for the past four months.

Not that I need any more proof of this ignorance, but it should be noted that they celebrate wildly every time we clean a water trough, because they are enthralled with the jug of Clorox. In fact, the toms try to mate with it. Of course, a tom's big, clumsy talons secure no purchase on the smooth plastic, and he'll go pitching forward off the jug, his beak sticking into the ground like a lawn dart.

One of the dogs' favorite games is to stick their heads down a groundhog hole, mirthfully hoping the critter will emerge for a good scrap. They know he won't, of course, but it's all in good fun.

Well, this game caught the attention of the turkeys the other day. They assumed in a very literal way—turkeys do not do irony—that there must be something down the hole of value, for all seven proceeded to stick their considerable necks down the hole.

They stayed that way until we all tired of watching. The dogs were particularly crushed, because, for them, the turkeys had just ruined a jolly good sport. Somehow, seeing another creature peering stupidly down the hole with the very real expectation of results just spoiled all the fun of it.

The turkeys get into everything we do. We cannot, for example, sit outside and peel peaches—or do anything for that matter—because the turkeys will be over it, around it and in it. I have this black hatred of them, but it does me no good. You cannot get mad at a turkey, any more than you can get angry with a tomato plant.

You can't scream at them, because they do not care. You can't kick or otherwise disable them, because they have value; heritage turkeys bring prime prices at Thanksgiving.

But I do know this: This Thanksgiving, no one will be more thankful than I am.

There appears to be a pecking order between rooster and turkeys
October 6, 2010

The life and times of Chuckles the cowardly rooster are almost too painful to chronicle, at least for anyone who believes that any child of nature ought to be blessed with a little confidence.

As has been reported here before, Chuckles was saved from the butcher block by pretending to be a hen for a solid eight weeks. But the day after the other roosters in the hatch were shipped off to the processor, "she"—much to our astonishment—stood up and crowed.

Chuckles kept his head, but in the process lost any modicum of self respect. The results, for him, have been kind of a wash. The balance of his life to date has been spent in full flight, sprinting away from enemies real or imagined, shrieking at the top of his lungs in a girly, high-pitched cackle of alarm.

Frankly, we were kind of ashamed to have him around the place. We tried to give him away, but there were no takers. And we have a rule around Little Farm by the Creek—once an animal has a name, it cannot be eaten.

His name was drawn from his appearance. Pure white, he has no tail, but it almost seems as if his tail feathers instead popped out on both sides of his neck and twirled skyward like some grotesquely overgrown handlebar mustache. An optimist would say it's distinguished. A pessimist would say it's sort of like feathered acne.

After reading this description a time or two, local artist Beth Mills decided that Chuckles might be a good candidate for immortalizing on canvas. At first I was dubious. A formal portrait of—of Chuckles? This seemed a bit incongruous, like Rembrandt doing a portrait of Red Skelton.

But Beth said it was for a good cause, benefiting the Humane Society. It's Howard's fifth annual Art for the Animals affair, and it works like this: Artists buy 5x7 canvases for a $1 contribution and paint an oil, which they return to Howard's Arts and Frames on Dual Highway. Howard's will frame the work and put it on display, where the public may bid, silent auction style, from Oct. 9 to 27, proceeds again benefiting the Humane Society.

So I sent Beth a picture of Chuckles. (It wasn't easy to capture a frontal image, since he's always running away from something.) She did a marvelous rendition of the bird, which of course will be part of the auction at Howard's.

But here's the weird part that even Beth at this point does not know —the part that can only add to the Legend of Chuckles.

A couple of days after being immortalized on canvas, I saw Chuckles in the parking lot in an unfamiliar attitude—that is, he was not running away from anything. Indeed, square in front of him were four of our free-range turkeys, each of which would have outweighed Chuckles by 20 pounds. And Chuckles, believe it or not, was fighting. He did a whole kung fu-rooster routine, whaling away at the toms with his spurs and driving them back in—well, fear would be the wrong word, but maybe with a tad of, dare I say, respect for the maligned chicken.

It was about the darndest thing I'd ever seen, and the only thing I could figure was that Chuckles somehow understood that he had become a hero in art and now had a reputation to preserve.

For several days, I saw the rooster in a new light. His crows seemed louder, his gaze more fierce. Perhaps I had a real-for-sure warrior on my hands, one who would stand up to barnyard bullies.

Then I looked out the window this week to see Chuckles running full speed from behind a barn, screaming his lungs out. A half-beat later, here came seven turkeys in hot pursuit.

In a way, it was kind of nice for things to back to normal.

British invasion brings changes in pig culture
October 20, 2010

For pure society, it's hard to beat a pig. They are always monumentally happy to see you coming, partly because you might be coming to throw them a rotting pumpkin and partly because they're just happy to see you.

If you don't read much about the hog named Magellan in this space, it's because he's never any trouble. He's polite to a fault, and to this day remains the only animal on the place that says "thank you" for his food. He'll dive in to his hog pellets and milk, and then stop, look up and make eye contact, and issue a couple of grateful grunts before diving back into his meal.

We liked and learned so much from Magellan that we decided to get a pair of Gloucestershire Old Spots, an old-fashioned breed from England. So they kind of oink with a British accent.

Despite their impressive size and strength, pigs are easy to contain. One string of electric wire six inches off the ground does the trick. Although the current is quite weak, they are not into discomfort in any form.

The Old Spots are on the small side and grow slowly—so commercial agriculture has no use for them. But they produce pork as it once was, before the food Nazis encouraged pigs to be bred in the name of no fat and no flavor. At least that's the hope.

Right now, we don't even know whether Chester and Tillie have gotten funky, pig-style. Frankly, Tillie seems a lot more interested in eating than in any other recreation, and while Chester has thrown a few "Come here oftens?" her way, the fact is that he is also too easily distracted by foodstuffs to get to second base.

The girl is a lot smarter than the boy, sad to say. They take their suppers in two separate tubs and Chester—always worried that Tillie's food is somehow better than his own—chases her off of her bowl, forcing her to scamper over to his. At which point he decides that he wants his original tub, and chases her back.

For a while I was worried that Tillie might not be getting her share, but she will see him coming out of the corner of her eye and stuff three or four apples in her cheek like a squirrel and carry them to her new locale. And poor Chester, for the life of him, can't figure where all the food went in such short order.

The other day, however, he fancied himself in the catbird seat. At dinnertime, he was front and center, but Tillie was at the far side of the pasture, oblivious to my approach.

Instantly, Chester grasped the landscape—that is, two pig servings divided by one is a lot more than two pig servings divided by two. And he made a plan. It was in his interest not to do or say anything that would call Tillie to the table.

Normally I am greeted with ear-splitting squeals of happiness, but this time Chester only issued a few low grunts under his legendary breath. As I approached with the bucket, he looked at me, then back to check on Tillie's whereabouts, then back at me.

Of all a pig's assets, keen vision is not among them. So as C. kept scrupulous track of T., he failed to notice that he himself had inched forward, in dangerous proximity to the electric wire.

In glorious anticipation of his dinner being supersized, one lone strand of drool cascaded from his gaping maw and made contact with the wire.

By the time he landed back upon the earth, his blood-curtailing shrieks had attracted Tillie to the fore, to dine as usual.

Chester was in a black mood for some time after that, but after awhile, his natural optimism returned. He might have learned his lesson, but I'm not counting on it. To a pig, the siren song of slop is a powerful thing.

Goat love truly stinks

November 8, 2010

Names are interesting things.

When we take our poultry in for processing, we often go to a Mennonite farm near Waynesboro, Pa., where they also raise strawberries and raspberries.

When we buy an animal for the freezer at the Frederick County, Va., fair, we send it to a family processor whose last name happens to be Gore.

So there you go. You can wind up at Berry Blossom Poultry or Gore's Slaughter. I don't know if this makes any difference to the animal, but it serves as a lead-in to the fact that there is occasionally some unpleasantness in farm life and there is no getting around it.

And if I may say so, sometimes the beginning of life can be just as tumultuous as the end.

A female dairy goat is as neat and tidy an animal as you could want. She is far cleaner than a dog, and has much higher standards on matters of diet, if you know what I'm saying.

The same, sadly, cannot be said of the males of the species. A buck is a celebration of filth. A strawberry milkshake, or his own urine—as beverages go, it's all pretty much okey-dokey to him.

His face is a timeless reflection of debauchery, from his arching horns to his flowing beard to his perpetually bemused expression. His coat is a Merlinesque robe of coarse, matted hair, which traps and humidifies every last particle of scent that the animal has produced since the day he was born. And what a scent. A stink bug might be confused with a violet with only a billy goat for comparison.

If a smell could glow, that's more or less the first, eye-watering impression a buck will make on the caprine novice.

This is all a long way of saying that we do not keep a billy on our farm. You know the way everything around a small child seems to get sticky? Everything around a buck seems to get smelly. But while we might find the fragrance to be offensive, the doe, needless to say, will not. As a matter of fact, sometimes she needs that smell to get in the mood.

We have a half-dozen female goats on the farm, and none of them, of late, had shown any signs of coming into heat. This is breeding season, and you don't want to drag it out too long because birthing in the heat of summer is hard on everyone, most notably me.

So our mentor, Tracy, suggested that our does might need a whiff of a buck to remind them of the business at hand.

Since the drugstores in this area do not stock Bottled Goat Orf next to the Viagra, we took a quick trip over to Tracy and Mike's, washcloth in hand.

Sometimes you get yourself into a situation that you never could have envisioned at any point in your life, and I think it's safe to say neither Beth nor I had anticipated the day when we would be swabbing a nasty goat undercarriage with a cloth, zipping it up in a plastic bag, rushing it back home and waving it under the nostrils of persnickety doe.

Overall, in my view, it beats dinner and a movie, but not by much. (And Beth and Tracy might point out that they were the ones who had to actually go out to the goat barn, while Mike and I stayed inside and talked about weight lifting. But we were there in spirit.)

As it turned out, we didn't even need the cloth. The fact that we had been in the presence of a buck was enough for Heidi, who was ready for a hot time in the old town within a couple of days.

Goats have it a lot easier in that respect than the rest of us guys, so it doesn't necessarily pay for us to knock their smell.

Turkeys go to big garnished platter in the sky
November 24, 2010

It was a still Thanksgiving morning at Little Farm by the Creek. As the sun appeared over the crest of South Mountain, a thin mist rose off the stream like the description in a Thomas Hardy novel. Somewhere a dog barked.

No, that's hardly good enough. Let me try again:

Juliet the Siamese cat was the first to notice a paradigm shift at Little Farm by the Creek. While being privy to none of the day's transpirings first-hand, her keen feline awareness had somehow sensed a meaningful change ...

No.

It was the best Thanksgiving the farm had ever known. For the arrow of peace and tranquility had finally found its mark and pierced the beating heart of fortitude that all summer long had been so resolute, so unwavering through times of turmoil, so, so—so shoot.

I give up. I have been writing this Special Occasion column in my head for seven months now, and when the time is upon me to write, I miss the mark.

It's just too big a stage, I guess, too cataclysmic an event for me to keep my head. For the turkeys that have tortured my soul have now gone to that big garnished platter in the sky, where they can no longer attack me with their pointed beaks and ear-splitting gobbles.

I am aware that some people have hinted around that I must to some degree be exaggerating their obnoxiousness—that no creature could be so pathologically clinging, so aggressively stupid as what I have described.

Well for you, there's this little thing I like to call "YouTube," where I have posted the turkey's assault on a Clorox bottle, at www.youtube.com/watch?v=dioIOhAAqY8 (if that's too much, you can just search turkeys v. bleach).

Your guess is as good as mine as to what a Clorox bottle would mean to a gang of Toms, but it got so bad that if we wanted to disinfect the milk room or scrub down a water trough, we had to do it when the turkeys had been put up for the night, lest we risk a march of the psychotic drumsticks.

No other vessel made them so angry. No other consumer household product would even so much as get their admittedly limited attention. Bottles of Lysol, Mr. Clean and Windex were all safe. But Clorox set them off.

The only other thing that made them flip out like this was each other. Sometimes they got into such bloody fights it became a real effort to keep them alive long enough to kill them.

So you can see what I was up against, and what a relief it is to have them gone. I know there are a few animal rights people who may feel bad about eating a turkey on Thanksgiving. Don't. You are doing the nation a service as a right-thinking American.

The day before they were to fulfill their mission, one of the turkey hens committed the eternal sin of chasing Beth's bulldog Hannah across the parking lot. Beth is a forgiving person and you can do a lot of things that she will overlook—but do not ever mess with her bulldog.

(My own view was that an animal trained, however long ago, to tangle with a 1 ton Brahman really shouldn't be running from a female bird, but I was smart enough not to bring that up.)

So any last thread of sympathy any of us may have had for these miserable creatures evaporated like steam over a mound of stuffing. Pulling weeds has generated more emotion in me than crating up the turkeys on that last journey.

Of course weeds can't attack Clorox jugs, so the turkeys and I will always have that.

Bouvier des Flandres not the bravest buckaroo
February 23, 2011

Little is required of the bouvier des Flandres named Opie. His job is to be a faithful companion at home, and not embarrass us too much when we go into town. He does a pretty good job of the former.

Opie is generally a reserved animal—not the bravest buckaroo, Beth likes to say—who will assess a new situation thoroughly before he offers an opinion or engages in a course of action.

111

For this reason, bouviers are popular as police dogs. They generally don't rip people's heads off until they have thoroughly absorbed the situation.

Opie is like this. If he is confused about something, he will take a seat and watch until all sides have made their case. Of course, on this point, one could bicker about the amount of lag time that is often involved.

When he was a puppy, a UPS truck rattled up the drive, dropped off a package and left. Shortly thereafter, we noticed a distinct absence of dog. We assumed he chased the truck back down the lane, and we spent considerable time searching for him—until we found him on the back porch hiding behind the grill.

No lie, it's taken the animal three years to figure out that it's OK to chase squirrels which, now that the matter is settled in his mind, he does with great enthusiasm. I like to think he's not a sissy, just carefu-None of the above is an issue at home. It only comes into play when we take him somewhere, which we seldom do, because being out in public with Opie is only slightly less embarrassing than being seen with Brad Womack..

As soon as we get into the car, he (Opie, not Brad Womack) begins to howl in a most unnatural way, much like a feline caterwauling, but much lower in tone and louder in volume. It is punctuated by sharp jabs of a bark and yip, then back to the chorus. There's no real way to describe it, except that it is not a sound of this world and almost always makes children cry.

We didn't even realize the extent of it, until one of the doggie beauticians at Dogs R US let it slip that they thought it great fun to call up people they knew were not home and leave Opie's "message" on their answering machines. Apparently, he serenades his furdressers the whole time he's being bathed, which is kind of like getting a call from the principal telling you that it was your son who wrote "Push-Up Bras Rule" in herbicide on the school athletic field.

This week we took both dogs to the vet; it was hard to tell who was more ashamed, me or the bulldog Hannah, who had to share a waiting room with Opie. I'd even started to think that it might all be an act, but then when they came to take Opie away for his heartworm test, he dived behind Beth like a 19th century street urchin clinging to his mama's skirt.

The other unfortunate truth is that they say that a dog will begin to take on the personality of its owner. I've always regarded that as an old wives' tale, but just to be sure, I "put out a feeler" with Beth by recounting that I never howl or complain about anything, and I certainly don't run in the other direction when other people come around.

The immediate affirmation I was expecting on these two points seemed to be awfully slow in coming. In its place was a rather awkward silence, and one of those nod/shakes of the head, of which the meaning is unclear.

But at least no one has ever taped me for their answering machine. That I know of.

Economic recovery going to the dogs
March 7, 2011

It's come to this. We have so utterly failed to turn the economy around that now were are turning to our dogs for help.

"Frankly, anything that develops economic activity right now is good," Maryland Del. Dan Morhaim, D-Arf, told *The (Baltimore) Sun*.

I think we would all agree with that, so let's move ahead to Morhaim's solution: Allow dogs into restaurants with outdoor seating.

I don't have any special problem with that It's just that I have two dogs, and you would not believe the amount of effort it takes to get them to pay for their own food, not to mention lodging, health care or entertainment.

They are two of the cheapest creatures I know. They still owe me for vaccinations back in 2008, so if they're allowed in restaurants, they might hit on the staff for some free water and scarf up some fallen shrimp tails, but I don't know that we can count on them to, by themselves, get the economy moving toward a sustained ...

Hold on a minute; it appears I might have missed the point.

Reading further into the story, which I admit maybe I should have done in the first place, it appears that Morhaim believes it is dog OWN-ERS who will be more likely to spend money at restaurants if they are allowed to bring their pets.

"Now, when people are outside and walking with their dogs, they'll walk by a place where they'd like to stop and eat. But they won't because they can't," he said.

To reinforce the point, *The Sun* quoted Graham Baker, the owner of La Paz, a Mexican restaurant in Frederick, Md., who recently had to be reminded that dogs were not allowed, even in open-air seating areas: "People feel very strongly about being able to have that ability to dine with their dog," Baker said. "When the patio was open to dogs, we had people coming in regularly. But with the economy the way it's been, if they had to leave their dog at home, they were staying home as well."

We live out in the country, so I can't really relate to walking my dogs past a restaurant. I'm not certain it would even be possible. Our dogs are nothing if not task-oriented, and if they were to walk past an establishment that smelled of pork chops and decided they wanted to dine there, I doubt there would be much that I, or the entire State of Maryland, could do to stop them.

Aside from that, I don't have any problem with eating next to a dog. In Europe, they think we're weird because we don't bring our dogs along to the cafe. I do understand that there is a segment of the population out there that will have a stroke at the thought of a filthy, contaminated, flea-bitten hound lying in an establishment where people are trying to eat. Of course, the dog owner's answer to this is that he invariably would rather sit next to a dog in a restaurant than next to the type of person who would complain about sitting next to a dog. At least the dog is bound to be friendlier.

And then there is always the allergies argument. And I'm not totally insensitive to that point of view, but I've always felt that if people make your dog sneeze, you can always find a table off in the corner somewhere.

So in the end, I hope the bill passes. Just so long as it doesn't give cats any bright ideas.

Lower the squealometer to get more for less
April 11, 2011

This isn't a complaint. I like living in the country, I like spring-time and I like small farms where animals play amid the wildflowers in fields of green.

The problem is that things are always being born around my house. And while I was used to one or two new animals at a time, I was not prepared for the insurrection of piglets that arrive from a sow by the hundreds of thousands. Or at least it seems that way.

Since we are not allowed to have normal animals at our farm, our pigs are Gloucestershire Old Spots, which are to the porcine world what Philip, Duke of Edinburgh, is to humanity.

They hail from the British Isles and were almost extinct over here before being helped back to their hooves by the American Livestock Breeds Conservancy. They are still considered to be critically endangered, which is another way of saying that I am not allowed to string up piglets if they misbehave.

Which, of course, they do all the time.

I will say that our sow, Tilly, is a remarkable mother, and by remarkable I mean she gave birth all by herself without any help from me. This counts for a lot, in my book. I could tell that Chester, the piglets' father, was with me on this point.

Chester has the best job in the world, period. It takes him 30 seconds twice a year. For his effort, he gets room, board, a large pasture and all the surplus goat milk he can drink.

Tilly gave birth overnight, and when I came out to feed her in the morning, the only thing different was that her pig hut appeared to be squeaking. In the next paddock over, I saw Chester just kind of staring into the hut, not quite trusting his eyes. While unable to read his mind, I am pretty sure he was calculating how this new event was likely to affect him.

Men go through life asking two questions: 1. What will it cost? and 2. Will it mean any extra work? That's the place Chester was in until he finally decided that out of sight/out of mind might be the best policy. And, save for feedings, we've only seen him a couple of times since.

The piglets are cute when they weigh a couple of pounds and don't move around much, but at four weeks they are a hornet's nest of pork, in constant flight and constant argument, especially over seating arrangements at the food trough.

Piglets seem to experience no moral middle ground. They either are being treated properly or else being assaulted by the most heinous offense ever committed in the history of swine. They are never mildly offended. Should something dissatisfy them, they go straight to a full-blown, screaming at the top of their lungs outrage that is hard to ignore.

In other words, you can pick them up and pet them or pick them up and castrate them, and based on decibel readings from the squeal-ometer, you really can't be sure which is causing them more distress.

Piglet riots go on all day long as they chase each other all over creation and ambush their fellows from hidden locations. With all this exercise, they work up a healthy appetite and feeding time is when things really get interesting. One or two will stand in the middle of the bowl eating and taking up all of the space, while the others turn themselves into torpedo pigs designed to dislodge the one who is making a hog of himself.

Matter of fact, they seem to spend more time attacking than eating. If they would just sit nicely, they would all get more food with less effort. There's probably a lesson for all of us in there somewhere.

When pigs fly, they need a pet carrier
April 18, 2011

Like many people, there are stores that I've said I'd shop at when pigs fly. Or when there's another flood of biblical proportions.

Turns out this weekend I hit all three.

We are in the process of selling off our litter of piglets, which are now at about the age they will go to their permanent homes. Some of these homes are local, some aren't.

One of the little girls is bound for Florida, and because of the distance involved, she is flying Delta (I would have liked to see her go on Pan Ham). So we're taking her to the airpork on Saturday, but in preparation we needed a pig-quality pet carrier, which we could find only at one of those stores for reasons I refuse to openly speculate upon.

We got some groceries while we were there, and it was quite the experience—and I mean that in a good way.

We got behind a family of four, and the first thing the guy had put in their basket was a 36-pack of beer, at which point, his concerns being addressed, he clearly detached himself emotionally from the rest of the shopping experience.

He was still pushing the buggy, it was true, but his eyes were glazed over and his mind was long gone. If his wife had placed a giraffe in their cart, I doubt he would have noticed one way or the other.

We finally located the carriers, but there were too many choices. I told a store employee that we had this little piglet, see, and were had to fly her to Florida and that because of that we'd nicknamed her Janie Buffett (I threw this in to kind of break the ice, since I didn't feel the girl was tracking with me) and we needed a carrier, and we had its description on a printout, but I still wasn't sure I had the right one and could she help.

I appreciated her honesty when she said, "You might want to ask someone else."

Suddenly I was hit with an inspiration, and I pulled out my phone, which has a barcode app on it. I scanned the product while saying in a voice loud enough for Beth—and probably everyone else in the store —to hear, "See, I TOLD you it wasn't just a parlor trick, I TOLD you this might come in handy some day, I think I SAID that it was a useful tool."

I then looked at the screen, which told me I had just scanned a cantaloupe.

When we finally figured we had the right one, we left the store to discover that it was raining pretty hard. This is actually good news for the pigs, which treat mud with the same respect that some lawyers have for slippery floors.

But it was not good for our creek bottom, which kept surrendering ever more terra firma to the ever-rising water. There is, or was, a willow tree halfway down the meadow that had lived through numerous floods and reached a height of maybe 20 feet. Its main root extended for another 10 feet into the creek, and toward the end of the day the force of the water overcame the root's ability to hold its ground. With an impressive crack, the whole tree came loose and began floating, upright, downstream. This is the point in a Red Skelton skit where the wino looks at the tree, looks at his bottle, looks back at the tree and pours the contents of the bottle out on the street.

The tree sailed along slick as a whistle until it jammed into a cattle guard at the far end of the property—where for all the world it looks as if it will be happy growing for another 20 years.

Well, if pigs can fly, why not?

Darwin was wrong. Sometimes it's "survival of the most pathetic."
April 25, 2011

At least it was for one of our roosters who, against all odds, is still limping around the farm, even though he long ago should have been grist for a predator or a Crock-Pot, one of the two.

Last summer, we had a nursery full of baby chicks that were just starting to get their feathers when disaster struck. As you might recall, it was very dry, and a family of minks that generally finds plenty to eat out in the wild was forced to broaden its culinary horizons.

In two nights, they had wiped out many of the chicks, but one that got away was a Welsummer rooster, the kind whose stylized visage can be seen on any box of Kellogg's Corn Flakes.

He didn't get away entirely; he was wounded by the minks, and as he grew, he developed a considerable hump in his back and walks with a hitch. Naturally, we named him Igor.

So when it came time to "harvest" the roosters last fall, we were as ruthless as the minks. All of them had to go, especially since they spent their days fighting each other, terrorizing the hens and making such a racket I was afraid the neighbors would call the cops.

We called up a farmer friend of ours to see if she could help that particular week, but she said she was getting married in three days. That sounded a little suspicious to me; who gets married on a Friday? But she was free a couple of weeks later, so we prepared for the big day.

We gathered up all the roosters and put them in a pen, but one was so violent that he about killed two of his brethren before I grabbed him and stuck the bird under a wooden apple crate, weighed down by a concrete garden statue of St. Francis of Assisi. Beth seemed to think there was something cosmically wrong with that, but I was on a mission.

She let it pass, but did insist on one thing: Igor had to stay. Said something about him being protected under the RDA—Roosters with Disabilities Act.

So Igor remains with us to this day, poor soul. He tries to fulfill his roosterly duties, but it is a work in progress. When chickens mate, the rooster chases down a hen and jumps on her back, grabbing her neck with his beak.

This is problematic for Igor. First, he can't run very fast. Hens running away from him invariably will have to stop and wait for him to catch up. He arrives, eventually, panting and wheezing, at which point he tries to mount his target. But his balance is poor, and more often than not he falls off before accomplishing much.

The hens are fairly understanding. At least as far as chickens go, I guess. They try to hold still, but even with that, Igor will go pitching and yawing all about, as if he were riding a mechanical bull. And just when he gains some equilibrium, Stink will come running up and clock him broadside.

Igor doesn't know it, but with each misadventure of his, the safer he gets. We feel as if he needs us. And some of the slummier hens apparently think the same thing, since they will follow him around in a little hen harem that would make any male proud.

This was Darwin's error. It might be survival of the fittest up to a point. But somewhere along the line, a creature becomes so unfit that others take pity.

Don't knock it. This system has pretty much worked for me for 50 years.

Pigs have to be hogtied for photo session
May 4, 2011

I don't know how many marriages break up over swine photography, but if a couple can make it through a session of pig picture-taking, as required by national registries, they are on solid footing indeed.

Some background: Gloucestershire Old Spot pigs are quite rare in this country, as are many breeds of old-fashioned "dark meat" hogs that grow too slowly to be viable in commercial farms.

I did not know that going in, but there is something of an endangered species list of pigs, and the Old Spots are on it. So they are very careful about ensuring that all new piglets are properly registered.

As part of the process, the breeder must provide a front, rear, left-side and right-side photograph of each piglet, along with a placard indicating name, ID and litter number.

I never put much advance thought into anything, so I'm not real sure how I figured this would play out. I kind of assumed it would be like a police mugshot and the pig would stand quietly and hold the 5-by-7 card in front of her snout while I focused, adjusted the aperture and shutter speed, played around with the filler flash and such.

A word about piglets—cooperation is not in their playbook. They are rock solid both in their physical stature and egos, and they have a pretty strong idea about the way things should go. Unfortunately, their opinions of justice often clash with those of their littermates.

So Beth had the card, and I had a camera and a coffee can of pig food. I threw down a little food and yelled to Beth to hold the card 2 inches above the chosen piglet's spine, which she probably would have been happy to do if she hadn't been instantly swallowed up in a sea of churning pork, as all six piglets and their 250-pound momma rioted over access to the snack.

The problem with piglets is that they do not come with rudders as standard equipment. They fly around the pen like a balloon that's been blown up and released. So every time Beth would come close to having the ID card in place, some piglet would shoot up from behind and take out her knees.

I tried to be firm, but fair. "Honey, you're going to have to hold the card a little more still."

This might have been the wrong thing to say. I didn't factor in, perhaps, the detail that we'd just had 12 inches of rain, and the pen was ankle deep in muck.

The problem wasn't that footing was poor—just the opposite. Once placed, a foot couldn't be pried out of the mud with a floor jack. So my feet were rooted to the spot, but I'm trying to twist 720 degrees at the waist to follow a bounding piglet, Beth in hot pursuit, with the lens.

After maybe an hour we called a truce and went back to the office to see what we had. We had some marvelous photos of pig tails, ears, hocks, snouts and stomachs. Had we been able to patch them all together we might have had a perfectly serviceable piglet. But for the registry, it wouldn't count.

So we wound up carrying each piglet to a "studio" and shot them individually. This was fine except the signature, ear-splitting shriek of a piglet in transport.

But it had to be done. And all I can say to the members of the church that was concurrently having an ice-cream social next door is "I'm sorry."

Sometimes, one person searching is better than two

May 19, 2011

"You know, this could wind up in the papers," I said weakly. It was the last thing Beth heard before she disappeared under the skirt of the mobile home that serves as our offices.

She was wearing black tights and a do-rag, armed with a flashlight, knife and a towel.

I really thought it was a bad idea.

There was little chance, however, that my threat of someday writing about this adventure would have any effect. But it was my last-gasp, hail-Mary, final-shot, know-it-won't-work-but-willing-to-try-anyway effort at changing her mind.

It didn't, of course. Nothing ever does when there are animals involved.

This all started (dream sequence) in the winter when a tomcat started coming around looking for a handout. Beth thought she could—and make analogies to me if you must—tame this wild, dark-sided free spirit, but it was of no use. Every night he would eat his food and disappear without letting her catch him.

He was a smart cat, since he'd have been singing for his supper an octave higher if she had gotten her mitts on him.

One night he brought a chick with him. She seemed to be a nice, sensible animal—probably a goodie-two-paws, A-student feline who was obviously corrupted by the motorcycle-rider cat.

He only brought her a couple of times, and then she disappeared. Then the furry desperado himself disappeared for good, which greatly disappointed Beth.

But a couple of weeks ago, the she-cat—I'll call her "Geena" since that's what we named her—came back, hungrier and pregnanter than ever.

Geena was more open to Beth's overtures than was the tomcat, so much petting and feeding and cooing commenced—with me watching moodily from behind a tree. I've been trying to cut back on animals, not add to the zoo.

And at some point, Beth reckoned that Geena had added even more to the population, their number and whereabouts unknown, though suspected to be somewhere under the mobile home.

We had been feeding Geena canned food for about two weeks—or trying to ... our property is studded with bold, free-range chickens too numerous to mention, and every so often we would walk by the office to see Geena hiding in a vent and a hen with cat food all over her face.

We kind of had the cat's trust, but not enough so that she would reveal the hiding spot of her kittens. So Beth decided that she was "going in."

I don't know what manner of scratchy, deteriorating insulation and spooky, spidery ick is underneath the average trailer that's been in place for nigh on two-plus decades. I do know that this is where the heroic husband is supposed to say, "Stand aside, goode wife, for I shalt enter the crawl space and search for yon kittens in your stead!"

I didn't say a word.

Actually I did say a word, but it was only the above-mentioned words of discouragement. I don't know how long she was under the mobile home—an hour maybe.

I was in the house for most of it, but every 10 minutes or so I would come out and show my support by hollering into the darkness, "looking good," or "any time now, I bet."

"We" didn't find them and have not as of this writing. Beth came out spitting cobwebs but with no kittens. I didn't know whether to feel remorse or relief. We don't need more cats. But we also don't need anyone getting the idea that the kittens could be found if two people were searching instead of one.

Birds of a feather get stuck in stovetop vent together
May 25, 2011

Ninty-three percent of all males love these calls: The lady in distress who needs a man of mechanical ability to get her out of an epic crisis. But it should be noted that there is a small group—my group —that fears these calls like they fear the permitting process on a protected wetland.

We are the unfortunates who have no mechanical ability, the ones whose failings in the manhood department will be sorely exposed should we ever have to come within 20 feet of a torque wrench.

So as I pulled into the newspaper parking lot this week, I was more than a little rattled to receive a call from a dear friend who said that a bird had somehow flown into her stovetop vent and was currently in the superstructure above the range flapping helplessly. I know the feeling.

I arrived at her kitchen to find that her diagnosis was correct. Or half of it was anyway. The part about the bird was spot on, but the thought that I could help seemed rather absurd on its face.

I gazed into the maze of filters, dust covers, fans and electric motors above the range and gave her a quick analysis: "I'd call someone." She assured me that she had called about every handyman listing on the Eastern Seaboard and none seemed real keen on starling abatement.

She had assembled a surgeon's array of tools on the counter, so there was no way out. I told her I was pretty good at unscrewing stuff, but putting it all back was an issue. Still, we "went in," taking apart the dust covers, filters and whatnot, until I was stopped cold by what appeared to be a cylindrical motor with wires all over it.

I was on the brink of unconditional surrender, when I noticed something. And here I need to stand up and salute the engineers at Braun brand appliances, for apparently presupposing that one day a

10-thumbed bonehead might attempt disassembly. Rather than the standard battery of recessed nuts, lag bolts, compression screws and sundry hardware that amounts to a mechanical chastity belt, the motor was held in place by two simple rods and two simple nuts.

I pretended to fumble with it for some time before announcing, "Whew, wow, got it. Boy, that was a tough one."

Above was a spring-activated vent, and the loud rustling told me I was just about there. With what appeared to be a tomato stake, I pushed open the vent and sure enough, the bird flew through the vent and out the kitchen door, slick as you please.

I could barely contain my pride as I put everything back into place —which of course was much harder than taking it apart. Fans, motors, hoods, filters, dust cover. Had it been my own stove I wouldn't have bothered. My lawn mower only has 50 percent of its original parts, and it still runs. If something's making a noise, I simply take it off and pitch it.

So we get the metallic jigsaw puzzle all put back together, when from the hood we hear, "flutter, flutter, flutter."

There had been two birds. Why not. Once again, everything had to come apart for the second bird to be freed, and once again everything was dutifully screwed and bolted back into place. I grabbed my keys and—"flutter, flutter, flutter."

What had begun as a simple bird extraction was turning into a Chilean mine rescue. Once again, we went through all the steps and the bird, free at last, flew out and landed in the yard, where it was promptly attacked by my friend's dog.

I tried not to smile.

Cooped kitties emerge with Coo Heard 'Round the World

June 15, 2011

I belong to that school of people who respond to weird engine noises by turning up the radio. So when my office started making weird noises I cranked the iTunes.

This couldn't be good. It had been so long since Beth's unsuccessful foray underneath the trailer in search of newborn kittens, I was starting to believe in my own magical thinking that the kittens did not exist, or had been eaten by snakes soon after their birth.

We had a stray momma cat now named Geena on our hands, no question, but (thump) I was still holding out a slim (thump, thump) hope that there was no nest of kittens tucked up in the insulation of the mobile home's (thump, thud, thump, hiss) flooring.

As the unmistakable sound of rollicking grew louder in the superstructure under my desk chair, I could no longer pretend there wasn't something alive under there. But maybe it was rats. I was hoping for rats.

Beth had been a believer all along, of course, to the point where she was urging me to invade the crawl space with power tools in order to extract the kittens.

"I'm worried about them being up in that insulation," she said. "But I can't see where they are with those joists in the way. You could get in there with your combobulating saw and ..."

"Reciprocating."

"... Reciprocating saw and take out a few feet's worth, and then maybe I could pull down the insulation and find them."

"I think the trailer needs those joists to hold the floor up."

"Oh, one or two won't matter, and if they're breathing that fiberglass that can't be good for their little lungs."

"I don't think that ..."

"Well, if you have another idea, I'm all ears."

The vet had advised to try to lure them down with a bowl of kitten food. But Geena apparently isn't big on reading labels, so she happily helped herself to a second supper.

I didn't have a better idea myself, but neither did I believe an attack on the structural integrity of a valuable asset was worth it, in the name of comforting some furry vipers that probably didn't want to be rescued in the first place.

We were still locked in negotiations that made debate over the nation's debt ceiling seem like a school lunch cookie swap when the game permanently changed.

From a distance, I saw Beth pull back a piece of skirting from the office, and what commenced can only be described as the Coo Heard 'Round the World.

Beth was nose to nose with a miniature gray striped cat, which had been the source of the thumping I'd been hearing. Or a source of one fourth of it, as it turned out. In keeping with their fiberglass birthplace, we named the kittens Owens, Corning, Johns and Manville.

So Beth is currently going to great pains to civilize the brood. She believes that the key to taming any wild beast is food (hey, it worked with me), so the little monsters are being spoon fed, literally, in exchange for periodic nuzzles.

My own thinking is that if they remain wild, maybe they'll go off and set up housekeeping under someone else's outbuilding. (I am not the only one on the farm with that view; our tenured cat, Juliet, feels the same.) But it doesn't look as if that is to be.

So if anyone needs a gray striped kitten, the bidding starts at zero, but does involve prying them out of Beth's hands.

Boonsboro has the right idea on chickens
July 8, 2011

Three naturally raised hens will lay about a dozen eggs or more a week—more in summer, less in winter. For many people, three hens in the backyard would fully supplant their need to buy factory-raised eggs from the supermarket.

A hen will squawk when she's getting ready to lay, and chatter proudly after she has produced. Other than that, they're mostly quiet, unless alarmed. A hen will make far less noise than your average car-driving, lawn-mowing, music-playing, leaf-blowing, TV-blasting human.

The manure produced by three hens will make a wonderful side dressing to vegetables and flowers. If hens are enclosed in a wheeled cage and moved daily across a green lawn, they will put Scotts Turf-builder to shame.

Chicken manure will only smell bad when an overabundance of chickens are confined in too small a space, as happens in commercial farms. It's the ammonia in manure that produces odor, and that's easily counteracted with carbon—a handful of straw, or a sprinkling of sawdust, for example.

The Town of Boonsboro proposed an ordinance this week that would allow three hens to be kept in backyards within town limits. To me that's too weak; I would make raising chickens a requirement.

In fact, an absence of backyard hens is a fairly recent phenomenon in America. Time was, everyone had a few chickens, in town or not. In the '40s and '50s, backyard chickens were common on Capitol Hill, and there's a current movement to return to those lax chicken-law days of yore.

Simply put, keeping a few hens is something to crow about.

To a large degree, we've lost control of our food supply, and as such we've lost control of our nutrition. Factory-raised eggs are produced by hens that see no green grass, fresh air or sunshine. Color is a strong indication of nutrients, and many factory hens must be fed dye so that the yolks of their eggs will appear to be more yellow than gray.

Chickens that see the sun and have fresh grass clippings tossed their way will have an orange or bronze yolk that's lower in fat, has up to six times the vitamin D and has 10 times the amount of omega 3s as store-bought eggs. If you have cholesterol fears, have your doctor do some research on pasture-raised eggs (or grass-fed meat of any kind) and then get back to you.

Unfortunately, wholesome food isn't as cheap. It's the feed of the factory chicken that's subsidized by the government, so the product that's nutritionally inferior in every way will cost half as must as a dozen eggs raised the right way. Somewhere in the halls of Congress, this model makes sense.

Worse, the people who need good food the most tend to be the ones who can afford it the least. Giving them, and everyone, at least the opportunity to produce some good, healthy food on their own is a logical, forward-thinking thing to do.

I wish it were more than three hens; I would make it six. That way, you would be able to give a dozen every now and then to an elderly neighbor, or a family next door that's having a hard time. A lot of poor eating habits can be mitigated by a pastured egg. It's not a miracle food, it's just food the way it's supposed to be.

And chickens can be raised on a handful of corn and a whole lot of nothing. They will happily eat lawn waste, stale bread, melon rinds and table scraps. Believe it or not, they catch mice and they will gorge on stinkbugs. (Fear not; the egg tract and digestive tract are two separate mechanisms.)

Boonsboro is to be congratulated for raising the issue, especially in these times when so many people are so afraid of so many things. I understand that the knee-jerk reaction is to be horrified that you might find a chicken sharing the same block.

But if people could actually see the conditions in which factory eggs are produced, they would realize that it is there that the real horror lies.

Joyful, highly valuable, gorgeous, talented, smart, sweet and lovely kittens available
July 13, 2011

When last we spoke of this issue, Beth had just introduced herself to four lovely kittens that were the byproduct of a one-night yowl between two neighborhood strays.

The Tom was never seen again, but the mom decided to make herself at home with us.

It took a while to get these sweet, lovely kittens to come out from under our office building, but they finally did, thanks to Beth's repeated overtures and an estimated 3.2 million cans of cat food.

These smart, sweet, lovely kittens got the picture soon enough, although they were still reluctant to interact. One is very brave, one is sort of brave, one is sort of shy and one is Garbo.

The outside gig worked for a while, but our quest to find them good homes was drawing a tepid response at best. Beth finally decided that if she were going to find people to take in these talented, smart, sweet, lovely kittens, she would have to bring them under a roof.

This is the part of Beth's animal adventures where I usually find it advisable to make myself scarce. Love to help and all, but I need to turn the compost heap today, or I need spleen surgery or something.

This time, however, it wasn't necessary, since Beth sensed my presence might be counterproductive.

Apparently, capturing a kitten (even if it is a gorgeous, talented, smart, sweet and lovely) for the first time is some kind of black art that involves drawing a circle in the dust, scattering a handful of possum teeth inside it, chanting rhythmically and sacrificing a chicken before making a grab for the young animal.

So now these highly valuable, gorgeous, talented, smart, sweet, lovely kittens are using a catbox, eating orderly suppers and on their way to being fully domesticated.

Although I take it you can only domesticate a kitten up to a point.

Early Wednesday morning, I watched from the horse paddock as

Beth took a slug of coffee at the house and then marched slowly to the office to say good morning to the cats. She went in. A minute passed. Then she re-emerged and silently marched back to the house and went inside.

A moment later she came back out of the house and once again marched slowly to the office, carrying a broom, a shovel and six trash bags.

There was some poignancy about this pantomime that made me very reluctant to ask for an explanation.

Long story short, these joyful, highly valuable, gorgeous, talented, smart, sweet, lovely kittens had themselves a Very Good Time in the office over night.

Beth will never blame an animal for misbehavior, but rather will shoulder the burden herself. When a bad alpaca broke his lead rope, sending his skull rocketing into her face and landing her in the emergency room, she blamed herself for "having her head in the wrong place."

I'm sure there are some readers who think I'm joking about this.

So Beth's only explanation of what had transpired in the office was a rapid-fire series of "It was my fault for ..."

As in, "It was my fault for leaving that bag of kitten food on the table," and "It was my fault for not filing those papers before I left last night," and "It was my fault for not putting away that jar of glue," and so on.

So anyway, the offer still stands for anyone who wants a joyful, highly valuable, gorgeous, talented, smart, sweet, lovely and on very rare occasions, slightly naughty kitten.

An Elizabethan collar by any other name would be a 'Happy Hat'

Changing nomenclature makes Opie the life of the party
July 20, 2011

I've been reluctant to write about the reivuob ed srednalF named Opie lately—primarily due to Facebook.

Last time I mentioned Opie—and referred to the fact that he's not the world's bravest dog—some Facebook reivuob ed srednalF group got hold of the column.

These people mean well, I'm sure, but they come from across the country and are apparently unfamiliar with this column. So they all got together for an Internet chat and concluded that Opie's reserved nature must be attributable to the fact that he is routinely beaten.

I didn't care a whole lot; I've been called far worse—but Beth? Safe to say, if she could have tracked these people down, there would have been non-dog-related beatings involved, sure enough.

So to save any more unpleasantness, I stopped writing about the dog altogether. Then I got the idea that if I encoded the breed of reivuob ed srednalF, it wouldn't show up in their Google alerts, and I would be safe.

I hope so, because I can imagine the speculation that would ignite in reivuob ed srednalF groups if they knew that Opie had to go to the vet with a rash on his hind leg.

If Facebook hears about this, they'll think I've been bathing him in Mono Lake.

But the upshot was that Opie had to wear one of those lampshade collars to prevent him from chomping on his hindquarters.

From the second we strapped it on, a more mournful, miserable creature there never was. They make these lampshades opaque when they should be clear; it widens the animal's overall footprint, while eliminating his peripheral vision—and hence, Opie would leave a tornado-like swath of destruction in his wake, caused by the collar crashing into plants, magazine racks, cats, etc.

It was horrible to watch. Opie is a big dog to begin with, and with an added lampshade, the fully assembled animal barely fit in our living room. Whenever he'd turn his head, Opie would wipe the entire contents of the coffee table onto the floor.

We would take off the collar to let him eat and drink, and when we strapped it back on, we would try to tell him how bad we felt for doing it, what a poor boy he was, and we were so, so sorry.

Opie clearly fed off this and was growing more depressed by the second, until his morose condition was about more than we could stand.

Then I got an idea.

"We're going about this all wrong," I told Beth. "We need to make this a joyful experience."So instead of a collar, we started calling it his "Happy Hat." We would jump up and down like crazy people and shout, "Yay, Opie! He gets to put on his Happy Hat! Good boy, what a lucky dog!"

To my everlasting shame and regret, it worked like a charm.

Pretty soon, he was enthusiastically shoving his lemon into the collar and bouncing up and down, tossing his head in glee and having a grand old time, experiencing such a rare treat as this privilege of wearing a Happy Hat.

Every now and then, over the next two days. I would catch him in a rather subdued, thoughtful mood, lying flat on his stomach, head bent under the weight on the lampshade.

For all the world, he seemed to be trying to figure out what there was about this hat that was so happy. But he took our word for it long enough to get back to normal.

Or at least, as far as Opie is concerned, what passes for normal.

Selling the farm?

Farming proves to be too much work

August 22, 2011

I looked out the upstairs window yesterday morning to see the long-haired, long-horned goat named Edward flash across my field of vision as fast as his 14-year-old legs would carry him.

Hot on his heels was the mini horse Doodlebug, who was apparently in a snit about something and had decided to take it out on poor Eddie.

I limped down the steps (the right foot is still tender from when my half-draft horse mare Cappuccino stepped on it three weeks ago) to start the routine, which included, in no particular order:

Opening up the chicken coop to a stampede that must have resembled a feathered version of lowering the gangplank on an immigrant ship on Ellis Island, circa 1840; breaking up a disagreement among two donkeys and four cows over who got the grain and who got the hay; and being butted about six feet through the air by a hungry sow.

Farming has gotten to be too stirring for me.

And too time-consuming (e.g. we are so busy taking care of horses that we never have the time to ride them.) And too hard. How was I supposed to know that? Someone should have stepped in five years ago and told me that farming was work. Because work, well, that just kills me.

And it was work I didn't understand, like small-engine repair and barn construction. No lie, I was building a chick pen and it took me an hour and 45 minutes—45 minutes to build the pen and an hour to figure out how to load the staple gun. Turns out there are two (incompatible) types of staple; it's kind of like the VCR and Betamax of the staple world, I take it, and long story short, it's an awful feeling when you've used up a month's worth of profanity by the 7th.

And finally, farming is too expensive. I thought all you had to do to farm was sit back and fail to grow soybeans so you could collect the government subsidy check. But this year we were burdened with a fine growing season that all but wiped us out.

So the upshot is that we are putting the place on the block and downsizing to something that is more manageable for two people on the north side of 50 who want to be able to travel for more than six hours at a time, before we have to be home to milk.

So Beth and I have entered into a new phase on "animal negotiations," or, to put it another way, deciding which animals will have a place "on the bus" when we settle into new digs. As animal lovers, we decided early on that we could not be trusted with more than five acres because we tend to accumulate critters like grandma accumulates graduation photos. But we're getting enough land to afford the opportunity to take along a few larger pets.

Beth does not want to part with animals (mostly boys—just sayin') that have little value in the larger farm marketplace. I refer to these as the "loser animals," although I am discouraged from using that term at home.

Personally, I kind of shudder to think what this new zoo will look like. In truth, it might not be so bad; many of these animals have good looks, although they offer nothing else productive for society beyond the ingestion of nutrients and expulsion of toxic particulates. So it will be a lot like Jersey Shore.

We haven't decided exactly when we will be making this transition, and when we do, I am sure there will be other hardships that will take the place of the toils of manual labor. But as long as we can evacuate before Cappie crushes my other foot, I'll consider it a win.

Wayward boar hog turns out to be a lover, not a fighter
September 12, 2011

"Oh" is such an innocent-sounding word. Used in casual indifference, mainly, it's the verbal equal to the ellipse.

Except at Little Farm by the Creek, where "Oh," as it is generally exclaimed by Beth, is an indicator that the world as I know it is about to cave in. "Oh" can mean anything from the water softener sheared a line and the basement is full of water to three pistons just fell out the bottom of the pickup tuck.

So when Beth took two steps out of the office last week, gave a little start and said "Oh," I sensed trouble.

I was right. A lot of trouble was standing out in the yard in the form of the mountainous boar hog named Chester, calmly snorting up chicken feed like it was cocaine. His mate, Tillie, also had escaped, but (being the smarter of the two) she was easier to get back into the pen, even though she was probably the ringleader in the escape effort.

This left me to face off with Chester. Beth, placed in this all-too-frequent scenario, generally has two questions: "How can I most efficiently control this animal?" and "How can I most efficiently control my husband?" who by this time has blown his stack.

Fortunately for everyone, she had to head out for an appointment at that moment, leaving the farm to two massively ticked-off creatures, who proceeded to chase each other around for a half-hour.

And that's when Chester first saw Magellan, the massive pet Duroc (neutered) male hog that resides in the south pasture. I'd heard about apocalyptic fights between male hogs, so my heart sank. And sure enough, Chester bristled up and trotted over to Magellan's pen.

There, better than half a ton of porcine sound and fury faced off. To my horror, they stood jowl to jowl, snout to snout, tusk to tusk, and locked eyes for a full 15 seconds and then—promptly fell in love.

I kid you not, little valentines were floating out of their skulls the way they do in the cartoons. They grunted affectionately, and sniffed and nuzzled. Who knows what other godless stuff they might have gotten involved in if there hadn't been a heavy-gauge fence between them?

Meanwhile, way up in the north pasture, Tillie can see what's going on, and the poor girl was howling at the top of her lungs for Chester to STOP it and to get his bristly behind back home this MINUTE. It was too much for her, really, as she watched Chester and Magellan whisper sweet nothings, completely ignoring her tirade.

"I don't know what to say, Tills," I said as I worked on the fence. "He left you for a dude."

I'd read about this kind of thing happening in the tabloids, but never dreamed I'd see it firsthand. Chester goes better than 500 pounds and there was no way, no how, I was going to get him to move.

Eventually it was his stomach (he is, after all, a pig) and Beth's return with a feed bowl that did him in. I'd concocted about a dozen schemes to get him back—all pretty "I Love Lucy"-esque, in retrospect (if I couldn't get the pig back within his fence, maybe I could put up a new fence around the pig)—but Beth is better at this sort of stuff than I am.

While I was awaiting her return, my neighbor drove up. We chatted a bit and I mentioned the wayward pig. "Well," he said, "it's another story."

It was the truth. No matter how bad things might become, I usually can still get paid for it.

But even so, it helps explain why I want to give up farming.

Seemingly sweet cat shows her subtle fangs
October 3, 2011

For the past several years, we have had too many cats in our house. Then, earlier this month, we added a second one.

She was a stray who arrived pregnant and unannounced over the summer, and had four wonderful kittens that were placed in four wonderful homes. Two actually went to sheriff's deputies, so if you get pulled over by a K(itten)-9 unit, you can blame me.

But that left the momma, whom we named Geena for reasons that I am absolutely certain must have made sense at the time.

Geena is lame in a foreleg, so no one was likely to want her when they could have a fully assembled cat still under warranty for no extra charge. She's a gray tabby, the kind that's a dime a dozen, except that she is quite elegant, long and lithe, and fine-boned with an exotic face and two black "necklaces" around her throat.

As strays often are, she was appallingly shy, and it took Beth a solid month of work to even get her into our offices, where she and her kittens lived while we used methods (ranging between guilt and extortion) to get them placed.

Then, Beth decided, it was time to bring Geena into our home and make her part of the family.

The vote was 3-2. Hannah the bulldog was enthusiastic about the extra source of nutrients provided by Geena's cat box. Opie the bouvier is fascinated by all life forms, and watched her as carefully as if he were expecting her to cheat at poker or something.

The most vocal, and boy, do I mean vocal, objection came from the little Siamese named Juliet, who basically is used to running the house and to having her way.

Vaguely, I remember what sleep was like. Now, it's more or less just an act of lying on pins and needles all night waiting for the next catfight or horrible round of caterwauling to break out.

I couldn't help but feel for Geena, the young, shy girl who was brought into the realm of the fanged she-devil Juliet. Every time I would hear a dust-up in some far room of the house, I wondered how humane it was to introduce Geena to the dervish with the cold, blue eyes.

I became less optimistic that they would adapt—from what I could hear, Juliet would not rest until this little hussy was no longer under roof.

But then I started to notice things.

I would walk past the stairs and they'd be empty—then I'd glance back a half-second later, and there would be Geena sitting midway up, still as a statue, just watching.

I would walk down to the basement, and there she would be, sitting in her standard pose, staring through unblinking eyes.

At night, I'd catch a glimpse of her sitting on the dresser. Or I would go into the bathroom or kitchen and she'd be there.

Then, over the weekend, I was watching a game when Juliet sprinted across the living room and dove under my chair. A flash later came Geena in hot pursuit, and Juliet wailed in grief as Geena took a couple of shots at the older cat before she saw me and started, before clasping her hands behind her back and whistling nonchalantly as she strolled out of the room.

All of a sudden, the truth hit me. It was Geena, not Juliet, who was the aggressor. And we didn't have a cat; we had Chucky.

I don't know how this is going to work out. Geena comes across as being a very sweet cat, but now that I have seen a window into the truth, a cold finger presses against my heart every time I catch her sitting and staring at me.

I'm thinking Opie is right to keep his eye on her.

Thanksgiving is a day for begging dogs
November 24, 2011

It is only natural that at bountiful tables across this great land of ours today, thoughts will inevitably turn to begging, and those who do not have what we enjoy.

We try not to think about it, but we must. We know it's out there, even if we do not look.

The hungry eyes.

The pleading.

The sense of utter dependency on the good will of man.

So what to do? Do you slip Rex a little piece of turkey under the table or not?

Most dog owners I know have a standard policy: They would never, ever, ever feed their own dogs at the table because they are worried about the precedent it will set.

But at someone else's table, they will stuff the equivalent of a side of rhinoceros into the grateful jaws of the family pooch, knowing they will not have to deal with the consequences.

Our own two dogs could not be more different where begging is concerned.

Hannah is a 10-year-old bulldog who does not subscribe to traditional forms of begging—which, frankly, would be beneath her. Instead, her strategy operates on the formula that humans, through the course of a year, will drop X pounds of food from the table unintentionally. It might not be a lot at any given meal, but as the months roll by it adds up, and Hannah has time.

With this in mind, the animal, who appears to be half catfish, will affix her lips to the floors, and with the power of a wet-dry vac, slurp and snort across the hardwood, sucking up even rumors of food.

It is quite a sound, really, and not everyone finds it appetizing. In fact, this might be part of the plan since more than one person has been known to push aside her plate as Hannah's nasal/esophageal complex—never the quietest of organisms in the best of circumstances—expand and contract like watery bellows, surrounding minute food particles with mass quantities of gurgling mucosa.

On the other hand, the bouvier de Flanders named Opie could not be quieter and more polite. But in some cases, this is even worse, since he uses—guilt.

The guards at Buckingham Palace have gained a reputation for patience and stoicism, but next to Opie, they are more animated than Rachael Ray. Opie will plant himself 3 feet 6 inches away, square in his victim's field of vision.

That's it. He doesn't paw, doesn't whimper, doesn't jump—just stares.

A Japanese tsunami could not move him. A can of pepper spray would not make him blink. His stare will begin to burn after a while, and the diner will find himself adjusting his chair so the dog is no longer directly in his field of vision. You can still feel him looking, though.

And, eventually, he will get up and move a couple of feet to the right or left so he is once again solidly within your general view. I know, it doesn't sound particularly offensive, but you try to eat a meal with a couple of eyes bearing their way through your skull.

Opie is messing with your head, and he knows it. He knows: One, he is within the letter of the law, so you can't yell at him. Really, what are you going to say? "Bad dog, don't look at me. Don't you have a squirrel to chase or something?" Two, he knows that pretty soon you're going to start thinking. You're going to start thinking about how the dog can have such unwavering trust in you. You're going to think that he has such faith in the goodness of your soul that he does not even seem to consider it an option that you will fail to feed him.

With me, it always works. You can do anything you want to me, just don't make me feel nice.

Actually, my diet at actually getting rid of actually not an actual success, actually
January 30, 2012

I am on an "actually" diet. I've dropped about 16 actuallys a week, but still have another 20 actuallys to go.

There's always a wake-up call, like when your fat jeans don't fit; you know something's got to be done. And my "actually" problem was no exception. The first tip came when I heard a co-worker who has been sentenced to transcribe "Mail Call" grousing mildly about how the word "actually" has become the kudzu of the English language.

It's getting to be a lot like "really," which as words go is little more than a grunt with consonants.

I agreed with my coworker wholeheartedly, until a self-conscious twitch took hold behind my left ear. Something I had noticed a month previous, but blown off as an irrational worry, was now raising its ugly head (flash to dream sequence).

Two months ago, a *Herald-Mail* correspondent was good enough to do a story and film a video clip at our farm announcing publication of my new book *Strange and Obscure Stories of the Civil War.*

In truth, the video portion of the interview came as a surprise, but I did my best. I put it out of mind for a time, but maybe a couple of weeks later I remembered the video and wondered how it had turned out, so I called it up.

There were some problems.

Most notably, was that in telling a story about the Confederates' movements prior to Antietam, I must have used the word "actually" an average of six times a minute. It wasn't exactly an "oops" moment, but it was pretty noticeable.

Fortunately, I was bailed out by my alpaca, a big, jet-black boy who goes by the name of Copperfield. In the video, you can see him approaching behind my right shoulder, curious about the strange happenings outside his paddock. Over my shoulder, he peers at the camera as closely as if he's thinking of buying the same model for himself. Then, satisfied that there is no immediate threat—and right when I'm about to make the most compelling point in the talk—he squats and takes what seems like a 30-minute whiz.

Really, it was impossible to focus on what I was saying, what with Copper stealing the show in the background. I read that celebrated attorney Clarence Darrow did the same thing once. He ran a wire down the length of his cigar so the ash wouldn't fall away, then lit the stogie right as the prosecutor began his closing argument. The jury became so absorbed watching the smoldering cigar to see when the lengthening ash would drop that they missed the prosecutor's argument in total. I know it's really not the same, but ....

So anyway, there it was, right on tape: I am an actually addict.

Actually is the pork rinds of the English language. It sounds good going down, because it is a transitional word that can soften abrupt paragraph shifts, much like mayonnaise bridges the gap between bread and ham slice. But of itself, it is an empty word with no real nutritional meaning.

The problem that I face is that "actually" signals the introduction of a contrary opinion, and I go through contrary opinions like thin carrots through a tall vegan. I know, I know. This is the "I have big bones" argument of literary excess. There may be some rumor of truth to it, but when you're sloppy fat on meaningless adverbs, such facts are incidental.

The problem is that when you start overusing words out of force of habit, it can be awfully hard to quit. Pretty soon it just becomes a word you say when your brain is empty of anything else, like "awesome," "exactly" or "liberal elites."

So now that I've ID'd the problem, how am I doing on this diet? Actually, not all that well.

Cow jumps over fence, sets sights on moon
February 22, 2012

I tell people that I breed my own cattle—which I do, in the same sense that people who say they "remodeled the kitchen themselves" have really just purchased the materials from a home-improvement center and then watched as an unemployed handyman from down the street does the work ... usually in exchange for soup and a two-week supply of Pabst.

It's easy, but not too scientific, to turn a bull loose in the pasture, and then wash your hands of the project for a month or two. I tried this route with moderate success.

The bull was named Dan, as in Dan the Man, but he soon became known as Dim Dan, the product of being unsure which end of the cow to mount.

And, as pleasures of the flesh go, his interests were more gastronomic than romantic. The boy could eat half a round bale while the heifers were standing around drumming their fingers and waiting for him to get busy.

His offspring were OK, but a little Dannish in some ways, so I decided to improve the line by sending away for a few rounds of bull juice provided by a fine animal in New Hampshire by the name of Lance.

How they go about collecting bull semen is a question that I did not ask.

It comes in very long, very thin plastic straws that the vet does something with while I am busy averting my eyes.

So we now have a couple examples of Lance's work on the ground, in the form of a heifer named Lucy and a little steer. We normally don't name steers destined to be steaks (a friend of mine named her's

"Dinner"), but this one was born on Halloween, so obviously he had to be named Spooky.

Spooky is pretty much what you would expect from a bovine—a slow-motion kaleidoscope of grazing, resting and staring. A little animated when he plays, but other than that, pure Ferdinand.

Lucy, on the other hand, is a problem.

Lucy is into everything. She runs and bucks like a stallion, strutting around the farm, bossing everyone around and setting that day's cow agenda, even though she is not even 6 months old.

Entirely disrespectful of property rights, she has decided she is to be a "neighborhood cow," foiling fences whenever she discerns there is something on the other side that she wants. Needless to say, this is Not Good.

The other cattle will stand on the correct side of the fence and bellow at her—either calling for her to come back, or praising her moxie, I can't tell.

Generally, a cow is a lumbering animal that will break through a fence kind of like a glacier breaks through sandstone. So it's never too hard to find the hole they made, except that in Lucy's case there was no hole.

I couldn't figure it out, until I caught her out of bounds earlier this week and gave chase. She ran straight up to a section of the fence where there was no apparent structural damage, and I figured she had to turn one way or the other and began to adjust my course accordingly.

Instead, she simply levitated and jumped the 4-foot fence slick as a horse at a steeplechase. I stopped cold. I've seen a fair amount of things on the farm, but never this. All the heifers in the world, and I get the Celebrated Jumping Cow of Washington County.

There were a lot of things I was bargaining on when I got into beef cattle. But surrounding the entire property with a deer fence wasn't one of them. Short of that, it looks like the best thing I can do is bring back Dim Dan.

Independent critters are no organized party on moving day
May 16, 2012

Beth says that all animals are Republicans because they hate change.

They are wonderful, charming and warm until you try to alter the way things have always been done, at which point they become frightened, snarling monsters who likely as not will get right in your face and threaten to stampede you if you so much as suggest a single-payer health system.

But our cattle and donkeys were in for a major change Tuesday when they had to be moved to a new home—forget that they are going from a rather rocky hillside to a broad, lush river bottom surrounded by green, West Virginia mountains. No site can out-Heidi this one, but, of course, the animals did not know that.

Here was Beth's way of moving her donkeys: She parked the horse trailer in the corral and opened the gate. Every morning and night she would sit for what seemed like hours in the trailer, hand-feeding them grapes every time they would take an additional step up the ramp.

In this fashion, she was able to get them closer and closer to the trailer itself until, with practice, patience and attention to detail, she was able to lure them into the trailer.

Here was my way of moving my cattle: I called my friend Jonathan and asked him to do it for me.

Donkeys have a well-earned reputation for stubbornness, so we were certain they would give us the most trouble. But on moving day, I'll be darned if all of Beth's training didn't pay off, and they pretty much just walked up the ramp and into the trailer.

They weren't terribly happy when the gate slammed behind them, but that was their fault for failing to ask the right questions, in my view.

I was up next. My only saving grace was that I had Jonathan on my side. He is from an established farm family, and of an age where it will never occur to him that something can't be done. I, on the other hand, look at my shoelaces each morning and see a million things that could potentially go wrong trying to get them tied.

Jonathan has a stock trailer large enough to be considered adequate living quarters for an entire soccer league in some Third World countries. But he whips it around tight places like it's a snowboard or something, so he had it backed up to the gate in no time.

It was then that my lack of an off-season training regimen began to show in ways that would prove to be an embarrassment.

My theory was that the two level-headed bell cows, Cleopatra and Heifertiti, would set the tone for the younger members of the clan by calmly stepping on the trailer.

I had that half right. They certainly set the tone by immediately freaking and sending panic rippling through their children, nieces and nephews. And, for that matter, me.

When they burst through a gate like hamburger gone wild, I thought the jig was up. They zigged, zagged, pitched and rolled, sweeping away everything in their path for about 45 minutes. Jonathan however remained calm—this was obviously not his first rodeo—and managed to win by attrition.

But at what cost? Eyes bulging, tongue swollen, coat soaked in sweat, covered in grime and excrement, traumatized for life probably —and that was just me, I couldn't even imagine what the cows were going through.

But I do know that the Democrats are lucky that cows can't vote.

Hattie is no chicken little
May 28, 2012

Hattie turns 3 years old this spring. Or maybe it's 4. These days, I lose track. In chicken years, I suppose she's nearing retirement age, and she kind of shows it—a little broad in the beam, sharply critical of the younger generation and more opinionated than she probably has cause to be, considering that she has never been off the farm. She's a barred rock, meaning her color is salt and pepper, crested with a blood-red comb and an eye as accusingly sharp as one trying to pick the purse snatcher out of a police lineup.

I understand that it's a bit ridiculous to use the word "remarkable" and "chicken" in the same sentence, but literally from the day she was hatched, Hattie has been different. If you're raising chicks at home, it's common to get 25 in a batch, shipped by U.S. mail. They are called "peeps," and if you need an explanation, ask any bug-eyed postal employee who has been subjected to a 90-minute serenade of high-pitched chirping first thing in the morning.

Peeps arrive this time of year, and they need warmth—a gooseneck lamp bent over a cardboard box will do, although some people get a lot more elaborate. We used a heat lamp hanging over a low wooden box, big enough to house them until they graduate to somewhat larger confines.

When we—and by "we" I mean "Beth"—showed up to feed that first batch we got some years ago, all the peeps scurried into one corner of the box, as far as they could get from any possible human contact.

Except for Hattie. As the other chicks cowered in the corner, Hattie, all by herself, would march right up to the approaching human and stand her ground. She cocked her little head and stretched her neck as far as she could, showing no sign of fear or intimidation. Just one chick, standing all by herself in the face of a monstrous alien presence. This was sort of cute then, as I recall. Something in that slight little bird's brain was wired differently from others we have interacted with before or since. Unfortunately, she has become no more shy or respectful of authority as the years have passed. Quite the opposite, in fact.

I will be sitting in the backyard, feet up, reading a newspaper when, with no warning at all, I suddenly have a chicken in my lap. This sounds more precious than it is, especially when you have no idea what part of your face the bird might deem worthy of a good, solid peck.

It is also quite embarrassing when we have company. We have had critters at our place that weighed better than half a ton, but the one we have to warn people about is Hattie. Heaven help the person who fails to pay Hattie the proper attention, especially if that person is wearing short pants.

Of course people look at us oddly when we give fair warning over a bird. It's very much like the rabbit scene in Monty Python's "Search for the Holy Grail." In her defense, Hattie will squawk a few times, and then if her presence still isn't acknowledged, thwak. No lie, she has been known to draw blood.   Actual conversations with, say, the UPS man, have gone like this: "Watch out!" "Oh it's OK, I like dogs." "No, I'm talking about the hen."

The self-help chicken books are full of advice and cures concerning physical ailments, but they are silent on the matter of moral imperfections. So I am left with little recourse, other than to erect a rather embarrassing sign at the end of the drive: Beware of the Chicken.

Now that Opie's bite matches his bark, he's baffled
June 4, 2012

As documented previously, the bouvier des Flandres named Opie is not the most aggressive animal, which is normally one of the breed's selling points.

For example, where a German shepherd might immediately enter a melee fangs at the ready—killing everything in sight on the theory that the courts will have less to decide that way—a bouvier will literally sit down and think the situation through before choosing sides. Opie sort of takes this bouvier character to the extreme. He is a BDFD, or Big Dog From a Distance, meaning that the closer you get to him, the less certain of his bravado he becomes. His voice is as deep as a northern woods, and his gaping maw populated with white spikes is the envy of alligators everywhere.

But he is the classic gentle giant who nurtures kittens (although he might wish I hadn't told you that) and seeing to the well-being of everyone in the family.

He even chases cars at a distance—parallel to the road, but about 100 feet away from the moving vehicle. What others might take for cowardice, I take for common sense; Opie knows his limits and is not about to tangle with a steel vessel that outweighs him by 2 tons. In fact, he gets in these virtual tussles with pretty much anything that moves, conquering them in his mind and at a safe distance. This swagger and chest thumping applies to the animals of the forest as well. He will thunder his dominance over a groundhog hole that, by all appearances, has been abandoned for two decades. He will chase squirrels, but slows noticeably if he begins to gain on them. Once they have scooted up a tree, he resumes acceleration and then, boy, just lucky for that rodent that there happened to be a tree there, or it would have been one squirrel stew coming up.

So you can understand the disconnect I felt when I noticed Opie trotting along beside me down the lane with one of his toys in his mouth. He is not permitted to take his toys outside, and as I prepared for the issuance of a mild reprimand, I couldn't help but notice that the hind legs of his toy were moving. The rest of the toy was mostly buried in his mouth, the size of which has been previously documented.

It took about two or three beats before I grasped the reality of the situation—this was no toy groundhog, this was the real thing. It was a clean kill by an animal that, for the first five years of his life, had never harmed so much as a hair of another living creature.

I looked at him, he looked at me, both of us speechless. In fact, he seemed about as surprised as I was, if not more so. He wasn't sure whether he was in trouble, and neither was I. We both waited for my reaction. Discipline? Praise? In a sense, it was like a teenage boy with porn. You would kind of prefer it not happen, but you might be more disappointed if it didn't.

The only thing I was sure of was that the dog was not going to bring his new treasure into the house. About the same time, Opie was deciding that he needed to bring his new treasure into the house. After that, we spent about 20 minutes wrestling over control of the dead creature, sort of like Linus and Snoopy snatching and resnatching a blanket.

He hasn't killed anything since, but now he knows it's an option. This is a concern for me and for stupid groundhogs everywhere.

Two naughty goats get away with garden mutiny
July 16, 2012

Gather 'round children, for this is the parable of the two naughty goats, and there are many lessons within the story that will guide you through life.

The two naughty goats lived in a beautiful mountain setting with two kind, benevolent owners. They had an idyllic existence, in a wondrous green fairyland, where all the swords had been beaten into ploughshares and all the branch banks had been converted into Dunkin' Donuts.

The two kind, benevolent owners always made sure the two naughty goats had plenty to eat. Every morning and every evening, the owners supplied the two naughty goats with armfuls of golden hay, free from chemicals, preservatives or high-fructose corn syrup.

The kind, benevolent owners smiled graciously as they did this, singing a merry tune all the while, and ignoring the perfectly understandable impulse to wrap their hands around the little varmints' throats for eating them out of house and home.

In addition, the kind, benevolent owners would spend hours in the hot sun, putting up new fence in fair meadow and fragrant wood, openingup many the yon leafy dell for the culinary enjoyment of the two naughty goats.

The kind, benevolent owners did this with happy heart and without complaint. Well, one of them did anyway. The other one was, if the truth were known, pretty fed up with the entire situation, but he kept his mouth shut, not wanting to be on the receiving end of ye merry olde staff over the melon.

Of course, tending goats was not the only pursuit of the kind, benevolent owners. They also tended fine gardens of silver bells and cockleshells and tomatoes, green beans, eggplant, onions, beets, etc.

They loved sharing their goodly produce with all comers, who would gratefully express their thanks for the tomatoes, onions and beans, although they would usually say, "don't worry quite so much about the cockleshells next time around."

With all the bounty of the land, you would assume that man and beast alike would be content with their lot and while away the hours strumming on the lute, or hay rack or what have you. You would assume so, but no.

Rather, the two naughty goats bided their time until they discerned a short in ye olde electric fence, at which point they made a break for it, and this would be at 9:30 at night, so the scum had the cover of dark in their favor.

Now it came to pass that the bounty of the owners' gardens in the wondrous fairyland had been overstated by just a skosh. The ripe, sun-warmed produce was but a figment of the imagination at this point, and although there were high hopes that something might come of the garden one day, about October by the looks of it, the green plants were at this point quite young and tender and susceptible to any kind of setback.

It also needs to be stated for the record that the aforementioned, neatly tended leafy glen more resembled a Burmese jungle, so it wasn't like there wasn't plenty of other foliage for a goat to choose from even if he had really been hungry, which the facts have demonstrated was clearly not the case.

Nay, the two naughty goats headed straight for the happy gardens and ate all the forbidden plants that they liked. And those they didn't like, they took a bite and spit out, much to the outrage of one of the owners, but not the other.

And the moral of the story is this: If ye want to get away with murder at my house, it helps to be a goat.

Decision making around here is going to the dogs
October 8, 2012

This is so quintessentially Hagerstown it almost makes me weep: City officials have decided to form a task force to decide whether the city can support a leash-free dog park.

We do love our task forces, don't we? Not enough to ever do what they recommend, of course, we just like having them around. It's a warm blanket for our public office holders, because it makes them feel as if they are doing something when in fact they are not.

No one's responding to fires? Let's form a task force, that'll take care of the problem. Want to wash your hands of responsibility for the old hospital property? Leave it up to a task force. Washington County is the only place I know that needs a Department of Task Force Oversight to keep watch on the task forces. But first, we would need a task force to determine the need for a Department of Task Force Oversight, so that tin can might need a good kick down the road.

But I'd hate to be the chairman of this latest task force. What are you supposed to do, stand up there with an easel and a pointer? "OK, everyone, let's start with the basics. This is a dog."

And where you go for membership on the task force is hard to say. For fairness, it seems to me as if you need to appoint at least one dog. I want a task force consisting of Charles, Emily, Philip, Susan and Marmaduke. Matter of fact, I'd like to see a meeting of the task force look almost exactly like the velvet wall hanging of the Dogs Playing Poker.

And, of course, only in Hagerstown could we take an issue as a dog park and make it so horribly complex that no one can tell which end of the project barks and which end wags.

As Bill Clinton would say, listen to me because this is important: This is a dog park, not the Walled City of Jerusalem. A dog park. You don't need to get representatives from 14 different religions to agree on the one true God. You just pretty much have to find some open space, fence it off and hang out a sign that says "Dog Park."

That's about all there is to it.

But no, we have to get all hung up on location issues, size issues, liability issues, noise issues, dogs traumatizing people issues, people traumatizing dogs issues and just about every potential problem this side of "What if a plane crashes in the middle of the park and one of the dogs grabs a pack of airline peanuts and carries it down the street to an elementary school where a child with a nut allergy gets hold of it and DIES?"

So here again we have a situation—like recycling in the county— where every community in the entire United States of America (yes, even in Mississippi) has figured it out, yet somehow it's way, way too monumental a problem for us to noodle through.

I'm with council member and dog-park supporter Ashley Haywood on this, because here's the thing: If I live in the city and meet up with a dog, I would much rather it be a dog that is happy and well-exercised than one whose owner has no place to let him run, and he's wound tighter than Howard Dean and just waiting for a chance to spend some unused energy.

Matter of fact, maybe that's the problem. We have too many citizens who have too much energy without the proper outlets for constructively blowing off steam. So when something, anything, comes up, all the purpose and drive that should have gone into something productive is used to blow it out of the water.

So there's the answer. Forget the dogs; we need a leash-free people park.

Holy Cow!
Can we get some cooperation around here?
October 22, 2012

Subject(s) 1: Two human beings with combined IQ probably in neighborhood of 250, with roughly 50,000 years of cumulative ancestral intelligence at their disposal.

Subject 2. One bovine, female, with brain the size of a lemon.

Mission: Move Subject 2 about 30 feet to the west, with the encouragement of Subject(s) 1.

Long story short: We've been at it for three weeks now, but the aforementioned cow is in the same place she's always been, with little sign that we will ever get her to the desired location.

What is so hard about moving a cow from one 10-acre pasture across a farm lane to a second 10-acre pasture, and why would you want to do this in the first place?

Funny you should ask.

This all began (wavy dream sequence) back in the summer when we began looking for a boyfriend for three members of our herd, including our legacy cows, Cleopatra and Heifertiti.

By September, we had settled on a wonderful Belted Galloway bull named Cliff, who resides in the Richmond area, and contracted for two months worth of his services.

Ideally, we would have thrown the C-dog in with the balance of the herd and allowed him to filet the beef, so to speak, to his heart's content. Unfortunately, this was a nonstarter, because among the herd are youngsters with whom a randy bull can absolutely not be trusted.

This explains the logistical situation referenced above.

If I were a real rancher, I would have adequate cattle-management infrastructure in place, which basically means something on the order of the Bastille, but stronger.

My vet, starting with the words "it's real simple," sketched out a construction plan for me once on the back of a feed bag, and 20 minutes into it there were so many gates and alleys and corridors and chutes and headcatches and ramps going to the moon and back that my eyes totally glazed over and the project was dead before it began.

Not to mention that it would have cost more than my entire small herd was worth.

So when we need to move an animal, we must fall back on finesse over strength, coaxing the subject-cow with feed tubs, while holding others back with electrified rope. Once in a while it works. It did with Cleopatra, who, for the past month, has had Cliff all to herself.

But more often, you will find that cows as a species will always do exactly what you want them to do, right up until the time you really, really need them to do it, at which point all tarnation breaks loose.

One heifer has been so totally uncooperative she has earned herself a one-way ticket to Four States Auction in the spring. Heifertiti has come oh-so-close to the temporary passageway that we erected between the pastures (walled in with a curious patchwork of pickups, gates and rope), that we still hold out hope.

Not that you would know it by watching us. Beth and I cajole and drive the cattle while frantically arranging and rearranging a whirlwind of electrified corral wire and affiliated hardware. One problem is that, because of its jury-rigged nature, none of this various and sundry hardware has a name. So we'll shout stuff like, "Quick, wrap that gizmo with the fratzis on the tip around that goober with red thingie! NO, not that thingie, the RED thingie with the round hoozits on its whatchamajigger!"

Cliff the Bull, meanwhile, gazes at this circus from the adjoining pasture with a passive but amused element of self-interest, much like you would watch the hibachi chef an a Japanese steakhouse.

Which is exactly where everyone is headed if I don't soon get some cooperation.

Last thoughts...

It would be inaccurate to say that today we are animal empty nesters, although we have downsized considerably. As mentioned in the introduction, our goal was to find an animal with which we were most comfortable and concentrate our efforts on raising that particular species.

For this, the cattle won the honors, and we have expanded our Belted Galloway herd while scaling back on most everything else. This was facilitated through a move to the West Virginia mountains, where Cleopatra, Heiftertiti, et. al., now graze in a spacious pastures alongside the pleasantly named Sleepy Creek.

Had we based our choice on personality alone, the dairy goats would have won by a mile. If money had been the chief concern, pigs would have offered the most profits. But the cows were also a lifestyle choice, needing significantly less care than, for example, goats in need of twice-daily milkings.

We have also kept what I call the "loser animals," by which I mean the males. These would be the older alpacas, boy goats and, of course, the holy terror of a mini horse known as Doodlebug.

I should mention that this has nothing to do with the size of my heart; it is because I could not have paid people to take these four-legged atrocities off my hands. Nor, to be honest, would Beth have let me.

So we all enjoy each others' company in far less frantic conditions, where there were so many mouths to feed that quality time with the animals is sacrificed.

And if these large pets have no commercial value, no urgent agendas and no expectations of higher purpose, the same could be said of me, and I think we're all pretty comfortable with that.

About the Author

Tim Rowland is an award-winning columnist at Herald-Mail Media in Hagerstown, Maryland. He has written for numerous history and outdoor magazines and news syndicates nationwide.

He is the author of several books, including the predecessor to this one, *All Pets are Off,* as well as *Petrified Fact: Stories of Bizarre Behavior that Really Happened, Mostly* and *Earth to Hagerstown* (all three published by High Peaks Publishing); *High Peaks: A History of Hiking the Adirondacks from Noah to Neoprene* and *Maryland's Appalachian Highlands: Massacres, Moonshine & Mountaineering* (published by the History Press) and most recently *Strange and Obscure Stories of the Civil War* (published by Skyehorse Press.

Tim is also keeper and lackey for a wide assortment of mostly non-useful, freeloading critters, aided as always by his trusty (well, mostly trusty) companion Opie.

Made in the USA
Charleston, SC
01 November 2012